Slightly Dotty

Slightly Dotty

KAREN MELLONIE

© Karen Mellonie, 2021

Published by Karen R. Marr

A CIP catalogue record for this book is available from the British Library.

ISBN 978-1-9989949-0-8

Book layout and cover design by Clare Brayshaw

Cover images © Steve Mann, Aliaksandr Narovski, M Hilmi Musyafa and Psartdesignstudio | Dreamstime.co.uk

Prepared and printed by:

York Publishing Services Ltd
64 Hallfield Road
Layerthorpe
York YO31 7ZQ

Tel: 01904 431213

Website: www.yps-publishing.co.uk

I dedicate this memoir to Vinny and George

Contents

Slightly Dotty

I never wanted to be a nurse I wanted to be a hairdresser and thinking about it I would have made a lot more money if I'd been allowed to follow my heart. But no doubt, hairdressing would have had the same result. Varicose veins and a bad back. Perhaps more money would have been earned. Mum was a nurse I think it was the only job she wanted for me.

So, I secured myself a place and left home at the end of August 1980. I clearly remember my first day and the following six weeks. I made friends for life the things we saw and did sorted the girls from the women. We all lived together in the nurse's home, a large building opposite the hospital the Royal Lancaster Infirmary and were allocated a small bedroom.

We each had a sink, and a cupboard, also the luxury of a full-length mirror. My bed was squashed against the wall, I could hear the traffic passing at all hours, something I wasn't used to coming from the South of the Lake District. My family didn't own a car so, the train was our mode of transport and I now realise, it was, and still is, the most luxurious train journey in England. The sands. The viaducts and for me, the homecoming. Hoad monument in the distance, growing bigger as I arrived then slowly reducing in size and disappearing as I left. Always present, always welcoming me home and breathing it's love over me.

"Keep safe, keep safe, keep safe", it seemed to be saying as the train gained its momentum. Anyone who has ever visited Ulverston will understand the Lighthouse rising and falling as you come and go, never failing to welcome you in and releasing you as you leave. Mum never visited me again in that nurse's home, her mindset was 'once you've gone you've gone, now get on with it'. And I did.

My first placement was in the old Lancaster Moor Institution. It was a very dark place full of ghosts, of death and fever that had gone before. It had a reputation. One side treated the severely mentally ill and was commonly known as The Lancaster Loony Bin. Here aversion therapy was commonly performed for the treatment of depression, or whatever else they thought would be helpful, the place was securely locked for the patient's own safety. The other side was for the old and infirm. This is where I was sent and was for the first time, in six weeks I was separated from my friends. The lingering smell, I soon realised was of urine and faeces. The old people slumped in bed, dribbling from their mouths, a sea of sadness.

The sister in charge was as bright as her lipstick, her smile more of a grimace. Her introductory words were:

"If you can work here you can work anywhere".

I quickly learnt to breathe through my mouth to lessen the stench, and after about a fortnight I stopped baulking every time I emptied a bed pan. The first job of the day was to go to each patient who had had an enema administered by the night staff and they were then left to sit on a incontinence sheet, in their own faeces, awaiting the day shift to come and clean them up. No offer of a bed pan or a commode, just a bodily release and emptying of bulk. There were 24 beds 12 on each side of the ward, each bed facing the other.

It was a military operation; I will never forget the pile of faeces underneath each patient as I pulled the covers back. Trying to stand the patient out of bed without smearing it everywhere. I soon learnt to scoop as much of it as I could into the bedpan, before dragging the patient to the edge of the bed and sluicing the skin and trying not to let it run into my shoes and onto the floor. Sister was a stickler for keeping the floor clean. Never mind the patient. After our shift we took in turns to soak our shoes in a bucket and rinse our tights through. It became our routine. We became our own family.

Life in Lancaster

My training was tough and strict. I recall clearly that when a situation occurred all students were thrown in. I quickly learned to manoeuvre myself to fit into the situation. Like most mature people considering their life in hindsight, I wish I could go back; I wish I could watch myself: how I coped, what I said, and recollect more clearly the many scary situations I found myself in. I can remember more clearly how I *felt* than what I *did*.

For instance, once in Accident and Emergency the Charge Nurse (male Matron) told me to go into a room with a lady who was obviously very upset, overwrought and disturbed. She was pacing around and talking loudly to herself.

"Hope he's not dead … can't be … we were only doing a bit of shopping … he was alright first thing … what did he fall like that for? What was he laying in the road like that for? … Silly sod!" On and on she went, and I just stood there; I was so young. So new. I felt as starched as my uniform and cap. The Charge Nurse never enlightened me, but I gathered the lady's husband had died suddenly, and she was trying to cope with the utter shock of this. I should have been primed; I should have had some guidance. I just stood there. With a little bit of instruction, I could have offered strong words of comfort and reassurance, and I could have allowed time for listening. I could have put my arms around her. That was it. In one minute, her life was changed forever. I let her down, but I was let down. I remain sad about that.

Another patient I clearly remember my feelings about, was a very attractive lady with a handsome husband. The lady was a patient in my ward. They were well dressed, and although I try not to judge people by appearance, I was aware that this couple had more than most, yet much less in a different sense. This lady was in excruciating pain; she was scraping the wall, the floor, with her hands, clinging to her husband, howling and crying; so tormented, troubled and agitated. Nobody seemed to be able to help her. I couldn't understand why nobody was coming to her aid.

I thought "Please help this lady. Please." I felt so desperate for her. I can recall wanting to recoil yet wanting to stay and help. I later found out she had bone cancer. This pain is beyond believable. Cancer doesn't care how affluent you are. These days we would use a syringe driver which is kind and gentle and extremely effective. It administers the required medication over a twenty-four-hour period, in a consistent manner. It's easy when you know how. I still think of that lady's pain. Being a nurse makes you hard though because nurses see life as it is. At its most raw.

I can remember when my boys were young, I was hard.

I am in tune with the generations that have gone before, and now as a relief nurse in a nursing home, I witness the fortitude and resignation of our lovely residents. I suppose what I'm trying to say is when I was young I was so ill prepared, and the general way to learn was to be thrown in at the deep end.

That doesn't happen these days. The students have their hands held much more than we ever did or could.

I was once told to get in an ambulance with a lady who looked alright to me, just normal, if not a little withdrawn. I chatted to her. She didn't once respond. We were taken to a lock-up institution in Lancaster and the staff were on standby to receive her. As I helped her down the steps of the ambulance her sleeves pushed up a little and I noticed both wrists were tightly wrapped. Dried blood was apparent. Then the penny dropped. But why wasn't I told? She was so unwell, and I had no clue. At least things have changed now, and learners insist on knowing and are confident and forward enough to ask. I've heard students say, "I'm not going", or "I don't do that", or "they said at uni we've not to do that". "I might get sued", "it's not my responsibility"….

There have been massive changes since I was first nursing and I hope my stories demonstrate this.

Human Nature

It was a treat to be working on placement with my dear friend Jennifer. This is her real name and we remain friends forty years on. During our medical placement we were told to prepare a dressing trolley together and to dress a wound on a young man on our ward. We were to use a solution called Proflavine, a liquid paraffin that was popular in the 1980s and 90s. Generally, Proflavine was the choice for packing wounds or any areas that had depths that needed packing out. This was 1982.

We didn't know him. We didn't talk to him and we had no idea what we were dealing with. I find this very shocking as I write it and I have discussed it with Jennifer many times to ensure that my memory is clear. She assures me that it is.

There was a new disease called AIDS. It was whispered about; it was something that affected gay people. I knew little about it, but I gleaned from the qualified staff that it was bad, serious, and something to be worried about. Looking back, the staff nurse who was instructing us shirked her responsibility. She didn't want to deal with it. She had inside information. She repeated herself: wear your gloves, put your masks on, and be quick about it. I also recall her sticking her head through the gap in the curtains as we worked so she didn't have to come in, but she was still overseeing what we were doing ... from a distance.

That poor guy. I understand now how he must have felt. I feel compassion for him now in 2020 as I write and recall. He was painfully thin, and his skin was so pale. He was covered in hair, yet his appearance seemed pubescent – maybe he was in his late teens. He was naked, helpless and it was undignified. He lay on his side and Jennifer and I stood on either side of his bed. I was the nurse who was known as the 'clean nurse', that is, the nurse who dressed the wound with all the sterile equipment. Jennifer was the 'dirty nurse' she dressed the wound down and removed all the dirty dressings and threw them away. In many ways I can see that the system from that time was much more efficient than it is today, and I still use the clean and dirty system. I say, "do you want to be clean or dirty?" It always raises a smile with the younger generation, but for me it sorts things out as I proceed.

The wound was an anal fistula. A fistula is an abnormal passage that has developed in the body and is a little bit like a small tunnel. It looked deep, about the size of a walnut, a hollow in the anal area next to the anus. It was malodorous, and although I remember the smell it was not something that I was repulsed by as I was halfway through my training and smells meant nothing to me. I cleansed the area as gently as I could, and Jennifer had opened my packs in preparation for me to pack the wound. We were trained to lay everything out on the sterile field in order of how we would use it. I used something called Ribbon Gauze. It was about half an inch thick and I soaked it in the pot of Proflavine. The colour was amazing to me, so yellow. The yellowest yellow that has ever been seen. I used my metal tweezers, as in those days to maintain sterility, metal instruments were used and then properly sterilized for re-use. Not like these days of plastic. (If only we could have foreseen *that* problem.) I packed the wound with swabs from my kit and, secured it using my Micropore tape. Every nurse had some in her pocket which, although handy, was unsterile and against the rules. But that is what I did. I don't recall chatting to this man; I don't recall him talking to us either. I do recall my feelings of discomfort, and of us wanting to get out of there the sooner the better, and of the staff nurse who most definitely had something to hide. She was unfair to us, unethical, and deceitful. We should have been offered a full explanation, and we should have had more support.

As with so many situations I wish I could go back to that day, sit down, talk to the man, explain about things, reassure him, answer his questions, hold his hands. But more than anything I wish I had a blanket that I could wrap around his thin body, ensuring some warmth and compassion towards him as I worked. I wish the staff nurse had taken me and Jennifer to one side and given us the low down on him and on this disease. I only put two and two together and learned about AIDS and then HIV years later as the virus became known, and treatment became available. The young man had not sought help when he first developed the wound. In those days the illness was abhorrent to people and the stigma and shame was too much for him to bear. People even said that this was a disease from God. It wasn't until Princess Diana really brought it to the fore front in 1987 and showed very publicly how we should be behaving, that people began to understand.

That staff nurse neglected her duties threefold. She was there to protect and teach her students, protect and help her patients and educate us all with her experience and knowledge and she did none of these. Jennifer and I were completely naïve and we were left in the dark, and yet I knew something was wrong, something was amiss. My gut, my second brain as it is known, was trying to tell me. I could feel it nagging me as I did so many times, and I still do today.

She let us down, we let our man down, and I will forever regret that.

The Wrong Body

The acronym LGBT, standing for Lesbian, Gay, Bisexual and Transgender, is mentioned almost daily in the media. Sometimes it is referred to as LGBTQ. The Q stands for queer or questioning. It is a community of people who find strength together to counterbalance heterosexist, homophobic, biphobic, transphobic sexualism and the conformist pressures that exist in the larger society. The community has identified and declared itself and is here to stay. At last people in some parts of the world who identify as LGBTQ are free to speak and act as they feel. Sexuality is only a small part of who we are but these days it feels like it's more than that to many people.

When I hear or read about LBGT and Gay Pride and celebrations of sexuality, it reminds me of a shift I worked in 1987, again as a staff nurse on the Intensive Care Unit. I was becoming experienced, I was learning. I was like a sponge soaking it all up, the older staff members would say: "Bide your time Karen, you'll see it". Whatever *it* might be.

My dealings with suicide attempts were becoming a bit more common, and my mind was beginning to be more accepting.

I cared for a young lady, aged twenty-one. She was slim with long hair, and smooth skin. I was always aware of people's skin as our patients were usually nursed naked. This was so that we could observe any changes quickly, we could be more observant with less clothes and clobber. These days paper underwear would be provided, but this lady refused to take her own underwear off; she hid herself and pulled the sheet around her. She was with us as a place of safety due to her mental health. Her eyes were huge. Wide open staring at us and watching us with mistrust. Again, she was attached to all the necessary monitors as she had suffered the humiliation of stomach washout in the Accident and Emergency department prior to her Intensive Care Unit admission. During the eighties The procedure of stomach washout was often used as a punitive measure. Even to this day I would need to turn away and close my eyes in disbelief at how dramatically and forcefully it could be performed. A large thick rubber tube approximately two inches in diameter would be inserted into the back of the mouth whilst the patient lay on their side and warm water would be poured into the tube from above. Often the clinician would have to stand on a stool for the purpose of gravity.

It was a humiliating and messy procedure; vomit would be induced, with the intention to remove any remnants of poisons that had been swallowed, thus reducing the impact of the self-harm. The patient may have ingested Paracetamol, opioids, tranquilizers, and once I witnessed a patient who'd swallowed antibiotics that were prescribed from the vet for a dog.

As soon as the vomiting had ceased and the water was running clear, the medical staff would administer charcoal into the digestive system. The absorptive quality of the charcoal was beneficial as, in theory, it would soak up any remaining toxins in the body.

9

Charcoal is of course black and would get bubbly in the stomach and patients would spit and regurgitate it for a few days post-procedure. It was horrible and I always used to think that the blackness of the substance represented the blackness of the mind at that time. I was always extra kind to anyone who had this done to them and I can still feel my overwhelming need to hold them or hold a hand at least; my empathy poured out of me into them. It was a disturbing thing.

My patient looked very small in the bed.

"Come on Ailsa, let's give you a little wash and then you'll feel refreshed."

She pulled the sheets protectively around her, only her huge eyes looking at me.

"No, I'm okay as I am."

"I know, but you've been so sick, it smells, and I'm sure with a little freshen up, you'll feel more settled."

"No, I don't want to. Leave me alone."

"Well, do you want a cuppa? Or just some water?"

"Okay, I'll have some water."

I went to get some fresh water, and, on my return, Ailsa had started to convulse.

My colleagues had run to her and placed her on her side, someone was bleeping the doctor and we held her whilst it subsided. I recall it didn't take long. It had subsided by the time the medics arrived.

She looked even smaller in the bed then. She was pale and had big black rings under her eyes. Her mouth was covered in the black charcoal mingled with blood where she had bitten her tongue. Once the emergency was over, I sat with her as she tried to regain some sort of composure. Her breathing slowed down, returning to a more normal pace.

The sheets were dirty, and I thought I would have another try to see if I could freshen her up. Just a gentle sponge down. She agreed then. I think I ground her down. I prepared all my paraphernalia. I recall in those times there was plenty of available soap, towels, flannels, even toothbrushes and paste. Not like now.

When I was ready, the bowl of hot water balancing on the bedside cabinet, I pulled back the sheet she had been so possessive about, and no wonder. To my utter amazement Ailsa was wearing men's underpants. They were well-worn, blue 'Y'-fronts. She had stuffed something down the front of them and when I looked more closely I saw a pair of men's football socks. Here was the reason she wanted to be dead. She was in the wrong body.

I left the socks in place and I never ever mentioned them to her or anyone. I felt mixed up inside and so tired. I just didn't know what to say.

Once I had finished and she was cleaner and comfortable, but with her lips still stained by the charcoal, I tucked her in and went to sit at the nurse's station. I pulled out her notes and read about her traumatic experiences. So great was her need to be a boy. A man. She had been referred to a gender clinic in London and her situation was ongoing. It seemed to me that her suicide attempt could go one way or another: to help her cause, or to set her back. I've never forgotten her. She was a desperate person, trapped, really trapped. I never saw anything as heart-breaking as that again. As life has progressed it's become so clear in my mind that people are born to be

11

who they are and should be free to do so. It's no wonder those in the LGBTQ community shout and scream and create and party and have parades and are flamboyant and loud. Live and let live, I say.

Hang me out to dry

During my four years working as a staff nurse on the Intensive Care Unit, I witnessed four serious suicide attempts. I came to realise that in truth it will happen if the intention is serious enough. During my working life, this rationale has been proven with evidence. Huge advances have been made in the understanding of Mental Health. Reflecting on this, never have we needed the service as much as we do today.

I was working the night shift. We had to work seven on, seven off. Some nurses worked their nights off, there was no European Working Directive in the 1980s. I hated night duty – it nearly destroyed me – but all nurses were contracted to work them. I used to try and swap mine as some nurses suited them, and of course in those days the money was better, not like now where there is little or no enhancement for out-of-hours work.

We were told of an admission of a man for close observation, an attempted hanging.

The young man had placed a metal noose in one of the sheds at his home and climbed up onto some boxes and tried to hang himself. Fortunately, someone had found him. I remember how thin he was and sinewy, with wild eyes darting around, he could not keep still, and I remember him being 'wired', by that I mean he was hyped up, restless, and searching. We had to keep his curtains open so that we could observe him from the nurse's station. All the monitors were accessible at the station as well as by the bed. I admitted him. He was monosyllabic. It was tough going. I made him a cup of tea, he wanted to smoke, this was a common dilemma in all areas of nursing and due to the gases, oxygen, nitrous oxide, humidification, Sister declined his request, escalating his distress. He rolled around the bed kicking the sheets and grunting. He got up and down and up and down. It was a tiring type of nursing. Mental health was misunderstood, and we wanted him to settle down. It took a few hours but eventually he did, everything went quiet from his cubicle and we could relish a bit of respite, until Sister asked me to go and check him. I walked slowly to his cubicle with trepidation. I thought I could see cigarette smoke coming from under the sheet.

"Have you been smoking?"

"No."

"I can smell it. Honestly, we must be so careful in here: there's oxygen. You could blow us all up."

"I won't…. I've had a pee. Can you take this?"

He handed me his urinal. It was policy to measure all fluids input and output, so I took it to the sluice and when I poured the urine into the measuring jug, two cigarette butts plopped into the bottom. Because I was young, I couldn't believe how he dare break the rules. I was amazed and surprised and shocked. I felt like that for many years during my career, now I am no longer shocked, just saddened. Resigned to the nature of us human beings.

Mr Hanging – as I called him to myself – kept us going all night. He climbed out of bed pulled all his wires and monitors out and ran around naked. We really struggled that night. Sister eventually managed to get hold of the emergency services from Lancaster Moor and they came and injected him with tranquilisers. These days that would be classed as assault. They took him away and I thought, "I wonder if I'll ever see you again." Little did I know.

Around two weeks later, I was on shift working late and I was going straight from work to meet my husband and some friends in the pub. It was Christmas time. I was late as usual, but it was a relief to do something my young self wanted to do. Get very drunk, very quickly, and laugh. The lot. The pub was buzzing, the decorations were up and the place was warm and friendly, a complete contrast from the place I had just come from. I was off the next day, I felt great. Everybody sitting round talking, engaging, happy. But when I turned to look over to the bar, there was a man with a deep purple mark around his neck. He wore a loosely tied scarf, but the mark was there. It was him. That man. I tried not to stare, but it was him. I looked away, all my frivolity gone in an instant.

I wished he wasn't there. I wished I hadn't seen him and, more than anything, I wished I was made of different stuff. Was I being dramatic? He spoiled my night. I couldn't ask everyone to leave and go somewhere else. So, we stayed. I was subdued, tried to have a good time and prayed he wouldn't recognise me. Of course, he wouldn't? Surely?

The week rolled on and I was allocated to work New Year's Day. The shift was fine – not too busy and no New Year tragedies. I returned home, had tea, got warm, and probably played Scrabble as we often did, and still do.

We put the local news on. A young man had drowned himself in the river in our town. He had made previous attempts on his life, the reporter said, and they named him. It was him. My man from the Intensive Care Unit, whom we assaulted with tranquilizers, who put his fag ends in his urine and who stood at the bar whilst everyone was revelling, happy and laughing; the man who dragged us through the night with him, restless, agitated, and mentally distraught. It was him. I was appalled and felt as though I had let him down somehow. I still think of him today when I hear of somebody wanting to die or trying to die. I wonder if they mean it. Chances are it will happen.

He's Nobody

During my years working in the Intensive Care Unit, I continued to feel very young amongst my peers. I was I working a shift with Janet, a Glaswegian girl. She was about five years older than me and she had her own young family. I liked her, despite her clipped and sometimes harsh manner. I felt she could teach me a lot. Until later that day.

Another attempted suicide. Janet and I went to casualty to receive the handover and bring the patient into the Intensive Care Unit.

"Come on Karen, lets go."

I followed, trotting behind her. Her walk was like her character – smart, quick and purposeful. Later, much later, I recall, my stance and walk became the same. Sometimes my husband will say to me, "Can we just slow down, Karen, we're supposed to be on a walk together." Then I smile and gather up. I say sorry.

The Casualty staff handing over were, I felt, somewhat scathing and this was unusual.

"Walkers found him on the fell, he'd nearly gone, should have left him there. Relatives non-existent. Can't imagine who'd want to be associated with him." This was odd to me, they usually made a decent, professional handover. They didn't even tell us the vital signs, or plans or anything.

"Come on Karen, don't hang about, let's go," Janet said. We walked together, pushing the trolley. An oxygen mask covered the patient's face, but we could hear him groaning, moaning.

"Let me go! Piss off you lot! Let me go."

I said, "Now don't you worry, we'll soon get you comfortably into bed and you'll get better." Janet glowered at me. Her scowl seemed to say "Shut up; you don't know what you're talking about." I didn't seem to be able to get it right that day.

Once we'd got him into the ICU and into bed, Janet left me to it saying, "Do his obs, Karen, and make sure he keeps that mask on." I duly did as I was told and I observed how bright pink his face and peripheries were. I knew that he had a lot of carbon monoxide in his system and this was one of the signs. He had driven his car up the fell and attached a tube to the exhaust pipe, wedged it in the car window and got into his car, wanting to kill himself. Some walkers had found him and alerted the emergency services.

I fussed around him and tried to make him comfortable. He was very restless, pushing the sheet off and trying to scramble up and out of the bed.

"Get off me! Piss off will you! Go on! Let me be!"

I said, "I'm sorry you feel so bad, but you've been found in your car and we'll look after you here, sort things out for you."

"AAAAWWWWW Just go away!" He was writhing and pulling at his face mask.

I stepped outside the cubicle; the other nurses were all standing around the station. I tried to listen to their conversation. They were speaking in low voices.

"Pervert, dirty bastard, the walkers should have left him where he was with the engine running. I would have." This was Janet. I listened. Then I spoke up.

I said, "He'll be ok. I'm sure he'll get right once the confusion has gone, and he's got rid of all that carbon monoxide from his blood and brain. Surely?"

"He's NOBODY. NOBODY. Mr Nobody. Nobody wants to be near him, nobody cares about him. He's a nobody!" She shouted.

"You've no idea Karen. If you want to nurse him go right ahead but I'm not. None of us are either; we've talked about it and we've decided. She pointed at the other staff standing there. "One day," she said, "You might have a family. You might have boys who want to join the Cubs and you'd expect the person in charge to care for them properly instead of taking them outside or into their car and abusing them. Sexually."

I can still remember the feeling. I can feel it now. A slow dawning. Then my mind went into overdrive. So, he's an abuser, the lowest of the low in our society. Does that mean we refuse to nurse him? Are we allowed to have a prejudice like that, so open, so blatant? Yes in the Eighties, we were. And the others got away with it, while I nursed him each day until he moved on and ICU was no longer the place for him. I admit conversation did not come easily as I digested this confidential information. It wasn't my job to discriminate though; the man needed care.

I went on to have my own family, a pleasure I didn't know existed. I had two boys. They were and continue to be the best thing ever in my life. Neither of them expressed an interest in joining Cubs. Things are different now and people are thoroughly checked.

Over time as attitudes have changed, I continued to witness raw prejudice. I saw medical staff pray over women who were ready to go to theatre for termination of pregnancy, and leave prayer cards on the trolley. I saw nurses refusing to assist with the procedure in theatre because they didn't believe in it. My worst dilemma was yet to come when I witnessed newborn babies withdraw from drugs from an addicted mother. It's tough. Nurses are human. But we must follow the Code of Conduct and the rules. That means we are ethically bound not to judge, not to be prejudiced, and, as always, to get on with the job. I started to observe other health professionals and I learnt there's good and bad. I decided to follow the good examples, ignore the bad and become the best I could be.

Epiglottitis

I was enjoying my fifteen-minute break whilst on duty on the Intensive Care Unit. Smoking was permitted. Yes, I know. Smoking in the staff room in the Intensive Care Unit! This was the Eighties. My generation. The ashtrays were always full to overflowing, and I can hardly believe that was the case. Not many years later when I looked after labouring women, a lady and her partner complained that one of the midwives smelled of smoke and requested a non-smoking professional. There, we had a hut to smoke in, where we smoked in all weathers, quickly between contractions, running outside pulling a cardigan around us, hunched up against the cold or wet, but compelled to smoke.

This day the Accident and Emergency Sister had walked round to the Intensive Care Unit (a rare sight). I remember regarding her with the deepest respect. She never visited the Intensive Care Unit. She never wasted any energy on idle talk. She was a thinker.

She said: "I think it's an epiglottitis."

For her to walk round to us and suggest this diagnosis was serious. She needed us to know and listen to what she suspected.

I heard the emergency bell, stubbed my cigarette out and ran. A six-year-old boy was coming via the emergency rooms. For some reason he was unable to breath and probably required artificial ventilation. It was medically known as stridor. Air flow becomes disrupted and blocked by something.

A frantic feeling started to fill my body. I hated it with a passion when the patient was a child. My anxiety rocketed; I could feel it. And I feel it now as I write.

"Karen, work with the emergency doctor; she is coming around with him, and his Mum is here." This was also unusual, parents had to stay outside or in the family room.

An aloofness descended on me, a feeling which I came to recognise. I became attentive and my concentration fixed on the matter in hand. I know it to be a preparation of myself to focus, be very calm, and listen carefully. I cleared my throat, I could hear myself doing it and I still do this when I am preparing to be on task, ready for a big event. I used to feel like this every time I delivered a baby. Almost like a feeling from outside of me. I was zoning in. This was the case throughout my whole career; I could become engrossed very quickly. I was ready.

The little boy came to us on the Intensive Care Unit bed, which the staff had taken for him. This was another indication of the severity of the situation. An oxygen mask was in place, and his breathing was loud through it; his little chest was struggling to inhale and exhale the air, his peripheries were blue, and he had a look of terror in his eyes. He lay very still. Only his chest moved. He was in respiratory distress. His breathing was a high-pitched, quivering wheeze as he struggled to inhale and exhale. (Stridor is sometimes called 'musical breathing'.) He was drooling.

We parked the bed where it had come from and the doctor told me to get the venous access trolley. I thought: "Surely, they've already put a cannula in? That's the first job in the Accident and Emergency Unit. Venous access."

I got the trolley and stood opposite her with my back to the little boy's mum who was trying to keep hold of his hand. He was wriggling now in discomfort and fear, I could hear him whimpering behind his mask.

"Mummy's here, it's alright little man … sshhhh now."

The doctor asked me to pass her a pink cannula, which is a large size. They are colour coded: grey is small, green is average, and pink is large. She took the cover off and I thought, "What is she doing?" I felt bemused. She hadn't even got her tourniquet ready let alone looked for a vein. I wanted to stay open minded; I wanted to say something. Something was wrong, as wrong as if there was a beached whale on my front lawn. It was unfathomable. The doctor lifted the boy's chin and told me to hold it up and then she stretched the skin of his neck. She had a feel around and inserted the needle of the cannula into his throat. I was astonished. A tiny amount of air was released, and the child's shoulders dropped, his nails turned pink, his fear disappeared from his face and his chest relaxed as air entered his lungs via this emergency tracheostomy. It took less than three minutes, from start to finish. I was caught off guard, and ever since that day, throughout my whole nursing experience, I never say never.

His epiglottis had become infected and swollen, consequently blocking off his air entry. It is a medical emergency and the doctor knew it and she gave him his life. He was rushed to theatre and a more traditional tracheostomy performed. He was given antibiotics and he got better very quickly. A vaccine was developed in 1992, and by 1994 the incidence of epiglottitis was drastically reduced and now is rarely seen.

Once again, I felt favoured to have been there, witnessing such an event on a random Tuesday morning. I looked after his Mum and made her a drink, and not half an hour later I went to make myself a fresh cup of coffee and have another well-earned cigarette.

"Be a nurse," they said. "It'll be fun," they said

There was a shift while I was nursing on the Intensive Care Unit I can clearly remember. It was 1984; I was 22 years old. It was before computers, only basic machinery was available, and four qualified staff to six patients was our ratio. We were waiting for an emergency. A child. Two years old. We were briefed that it was a drowning. This child had somehow got out of the back gate and fallen into the stream at the bottom of the garden.

We waited. And waited. Eventually I heard them running down the corridor and then pushing through the heavy, plastic doors with this boy, so little, on the stretcher, He looked lifeless. The ambulance crew, breathing heavily, shouted explanations.

"Drowned, working on him two hours, busy in the Lakes, couldn't get through, traffic's bad, his Mam is following." They were pushing his chest up and down. Come on, come on, come on; cry please, just cry! Nothing.

We were slick; we worked with what we had. We used each other and the equipment with efficiency, my leader barking instructions.

"You. Stay at the top with the anaesthetist. You take over cardiac massage, ten minutes each. You, you be my runner, if we need it, want it, go and get it. We moved the lights, handing over the laryngoscope, intubation suction equipment, intravenous access, monitoring heart, arterial and all vital signs.

We worked; boy, we worked. Time had no meaning.

Eventually the anaesthetist spoke up. "Shall we stop?" No output, no breath, not a stutter, nothing? Only death. It was a loud silence.

That lifeless, naked child. We stopped as instructed and someone pulled a cover over the little body. We all waited outside the cubicle until the Sister in charge, told us to gently wash him and apply a small shroud, make him ready for his parents. We did. We tended him, and made him look beautiful.

When his Mum arrived, she stamped and roared around the cubicle, she tore off his shroud and picked him up, she held him to her. She dared any of us to come near. She roared. And she roared at us.

"Get away stay away, don't you come near. None of you. Get off. He will NOT be wearing that". She pointed at the torn shroud on the floor.

It was a sight I will never forget, her wild, out-of-control reaction as the truth of the horrific situation dawned on her. She collapsed onto the floor of the Intensive Care Unit, holding her child.

"No, no, no! Don't even think about it; do not come near." She was saying it quietly now, under her breath.

"No ... no ... never."

After a time, as we circled around her, moving slowly and carefully, tidying a bit here and there and keeping a close eye on her, Sister moved towards her and bent down onto her haunches.

She said, "Shall we see if we've got any little pyjamas for him? We don't want him to get any colder. What do you think?"

"They're in his bag, somewhere … they're yellow, elephants on the front."

"Ok I'll get them." She sent me. I found them.

I said, "We want him to be warm, don't we?"

"He's got a name," she said, "Use it."

So, I did.

"Jack," I said," let's make you snug."

I now realise that dressing Jack with his Mum was a privilege. Looking back it was one of the most tender moments I have ever experienced. Slowly, carefully, we dressed him as his body became less flexible.

She picked him up again as soon as he was dressed, she held him close to her. Her eyes said, take him if you dare. I will kill you if you try.

Time went on. Jack's Mum sat in the cubicle with him, the curtains pulled around them. Eventually Jack's Dad arrived, hurried, harried and tempestuous.

Voices were raised and Sister had to intervene. It was 1984, there was no security, no help for situations that were aggressive and out of control. The last thing I remember is that the Police had to be called to take Jack's Mum, as she refused to leave. She simply couldn't go. She could not leave her boy. Jack's Dad left without her. I never knew what their personal relationship was like, but if they weren't destroyed before, they were now.

The porters came and Sister asked me to accompany Jack to the mortuary. We walked slowly without speaking. It felt dignified.

As I always have, I tucked this day inside of me, never cried, and never spoke of it again. There was no help, no de-briefing or counselling in 1984.

I completed my shift and went home.

"Have you had a good day? Do you want a brew?" My husband asked. He was lazing in the lounge. The house was warm and comfortable and my dog wagged her tail from the sofa.

"Usual," I answered.

Mr Polish

I have always spoken English, but considering we were a travelling type of family I should by rights be bilingual. I went to a French-speaking school in Switzerland, for two years. Now, as an adult, whenever I hear French being spoken, I have some understanding, and once whilst holidaying in the South of France, someone complimented me on my French accent. That's about the top and bottom of it for both learning and knowing a second language. My older brother is fluent, and I wonder if during our time in Switzerland, because he was a year older, he was able to retain the language into adulthood. More likely he is cleverer than me!

I recall an endearing patient whom I have held in my heart for many years. He had suffered a major heart attack, medically known as myocardial infarction. He'd been very poorly but was now slowly recovering. It's a funny thing, but when I hark back to those years it always seems to be the people who had occupied the same cubicle that I remember. I was learning my craft and becoming very confident with my work. I no longer felt anxious about my shift and worrying what it would bring. I'm not saying I was an expert at reading the ECG, but I could determine where the infarction had occurred. Depending on the result this would determine how good the recovery could be, and how much damage had transpired. I recognised rhythms and I could interpret this Mr Polish's native rhythm following the damage. Native rhythm is the natural rhythm of the heart. Following damage, when the healing begins the native rhythm will occasionally kick in on the ECG. In those years the medical staff and consultants would spend time teaching the nursing staff with patience and clear explanations. They would direct questions at us and I learnt so much just by being there. I absorbed the information. I couldn't get enough of it. I thrived on it. These days most learning takes place in the library on a screen.

This gentleman was Polish. I called him Mr Polish to myself. He had lived through the occupation of Nazi Germany as a young man and had come to England to make a good life. He spoke English, and it was a time when meeting someone from Poland was unusual. He was a family man; his wife visited as did his adult children. I spent a lot of time looking after him, and one day, he took his glasses off, and looked at me before saying:

"I have made you something. It is a gift for you for your kindness."

He still carried an accent in his voice. I was busy making his bed as he was now able to sit out in a reclining chair, still wired up of course, as all patients were in the ICU. I must have looked surprised; it was very rare to be offered anything at all from patients in the unit as they were usually too ill or perturbed and this would be the last thing on their minds.

"Oh, thank you! But we're not allowed to receive gifts; all nurses are bound by law not to take anything from patients."

"Okay, I wasn't aware of that. I'm sorry."

"No, no, it's fine; I don't want to seem ungrateful, but they are very strict about it. Sometimes once people have left us, they return perhaps with a tin of biscuits or some coffee and tea for the staff, and that's allowed and always something we love." I smiled and left him to rest.

The next day, the consultant came to do his round, and was asking about Mr Polish. I brought him up to date with the changes and ongoing recovery. He had his entourage of medical staff, who joined us in the cubicle. All the medics wore white coats in those days; now due to infection control, the white coats have mainly been discarded.

The consultant happened to be Polish too; the child of immigrant parents. I had previously attended lectures he gave, and his message was clear. He said that people who have come from poverty usually worked harder than those who hadn't. His work ethic was often discussed amongst the hospital staff. He was one of the youngest consultants in the country due to his hard-working philosophy and his background.

We gathered around the bed, to discuss the patient's current health, and how he was going to progress and move forward in his recovery. The consultant shook his hand, and kept holding it, seating himself on the bed beside him. When he spoke, he spoke to him in Polish, his native language. Nobody knew what they said, but my lovely patient began to silently cry. Tears rolled down his face. He held onto the hand of the consultant, as if he would never let go. I was so moved. The consultant knew that Mr Polish hadn't heard this language spoken for over forty years. It was, to me, a moving sight to remember and a feeling to hold on to. After Mr Polish had gathered himself, He said, "Can I have a moment in private with you sir?"

The other medics and I left them to talk.

Once they had had their discussion in Polish, the consultant came out of the cubicle and drew the curtains back. He asked if he could have a word with me.

"I have had a chat with Mr Polish, and he's made you this." It was a glasses case, hand made with scraps of soft leather in a deep mauve colour. It was imperfect, hand stitched, and had a little gold clasp which neatly clicked into place. It felt so delicate and soothing. My glasses were a nuisance to me. I would constantly be shoving them onto my head. On, off, up, down. I dropped them regularly and I was forever saying, "Hang on I'll just get my glasses." Mr Polish had obviously noticed.

To say I was pleased is an understatement, and I was permitted to keep it. I've still got it. It's very well worn, and these days I keep Paracetamol and spare pens in it and, oh yes, a packet of mints. All very useful for any nurse during her shift. I wear my glasses all the time now; it would be illegal for me to drive without them I'm told by the ophthalmic people.

It was a special, personal gift, but for me the even better gift, was the gift of shared language and the kindness I witnessed from one native to another.

Shall we be Midwives?

I knew that my time was coming to an end working on the intensive care unit. I loved it. I was thriving, but I looked at the older nurses and I could see how tired they were. Life weary. The shifts. The mind-blowing situations that people found themselves in, and the constant alertness. I felt like a deer chased by hunters' day and night. My adrenaline was constantly pumping.

"Shall we be midwives?" My friend Karen asked me "There's going to be a school opening this year (1989) It's called The Lakes School of Nursing and Midwifery"

"Well we can do" And it was like that, we were young and carefree. I shrugged handed in my notice and off we went. I would not have believed what was coming next. I should have given it more thought.

I hated becoming a student again. I was at the top of my ICU game, yet I wanted to move forward. At least I thought I did.

I hated not knowing the answers and sitting in a classroom with a doll and a pelvis, then a knitted sleeve and an orange. I felt stupid and naive. The sleeve cuff represented the cervix as it dilated, the orange was the baby's head coming through the cervix as it dilated. The cervix for those who are unsure (because I was) is the neck of the womb. The doll had a hard head representing the fontanelles and suture lines of the skull, to enable learning of the position of the baby. and the body of the doll was made from what seemed to me to be chamois leather, it was pliable yet soft and tough. The doll had a cord, attached to its body and on the end of the cord was a placenta. There was blue and red thread through the cord and placenta representing the arterial and venous blood. Later in our training we made knitted breasts to learn about feeding positions. You couldn't make it up. These days the students buy them on line!

I studied hard, and I remember saying to anyone who would listen that I would never study like this again, it didn't come easily to me I was more of a hands-on person I now know that my style of learning is kinesthetics. But I stuck in and when I qualified, I had done my own practising. I was pregnant with my first baby. I went to Manchester to sit my oral finals with a bump to be proud of. My first-born son has always been high maintenance and a perfectionist. Cannot imagine why.

I learned the anatomy and physiology and I knew it backwards, forwards and sideward, everyway there was. I believe the best thing about midwifery for me was that I was specialising. My knowledge and experience were consolidating. I was streamlining a singular subject. Mother and baby. Much later I learned that it was insular, and limiting, because although we were midwives and we had a special job, we only knew about one thing. Odd really when you think about it.

My first placement on the labour ward led me to many many sleepless nights. I thought that during my previous nursing experiences I had seen it all, especially when it came to blood loss. But no. Working in the labour rooms was like entering a slaughterhouse. The noise. The screaming. The swearing and cursing. Then fainting men. it seemed to me that the bigger the tougher the man, the more fainting he did. The rugby player chewing gum, the suave businessman dressed to kill, the builder in a shaped vest to show off his muscles. Down they went. I quickly got used to stepping over them as I worked. They didn't worry me, the slippery feel of the new born worried me (what if I dropped him?) the silence at birth worried me (come on baby cry) and the ever-present risk of post-partum haemorrhage worried me. The variety of ways people reacted to birth. I was extremely busy, I had some great mentors, and as ever I enjoyed working under pressure, the more balls I could juggle suited me.

Midwifery is a job for independent people. Most midwives I met were autonomous in work as in life. They were able to think on their feet, make quick life changing decisions, and I suppose we can be described as downright bossy and single minded. I include myself in this description. I'm sure my family would agree! These are some of my stories ...

The Ladies who knit

Every nurse and midwife work to the rules at their time of practice. They accept change as it comes and adapt themselves to an ever-turbulent culture. However, the body never changes, and of course, childbirth is childbirth and a woman's body will always accommodate the precious new-born.

When the time came for a lady to come into the maternity unit it was widely anticipated that she would have prepared the various necessary things that are needed for the baby such as vests, nappies, cotton wool and warm clothes, a baby grow and cardigans or little jumpers and hats, most ladies built a nesting box, ready for their new-born, whether these were second hand or new.

During my time of practice there was a group of ladies that knitted for the maternity unit. They regularly brought the garments into us and the staff could access a special box where all the knitted outfits were kept. All of them woollen, clothes of every colour, blue for a boy, pink for a girl, or if your fancy rainbow colours, stripes, or lemon, white, and green for the less traditional. All the midwives could help themselves ensuring, the little child could be dressed warmly. Small hats and little mittens, bootees and the occasional bigger garment for the baby who had fed well in the uterus, or had had a bumpy ride into the world, and the crown of the head, needed some temporary protection.

One afternoon the Sister in charge took me to one side, as I was beginning my shift. She asked me to care a lady whose baby was going for a planned adoption. We entered the labour room together.

"This is Karen, she's on the late shift, today she'll care for you and babe."

"What's your name" I asked.

"Shelley" she said.

Sister left me to it and I tidied round the room, all the while assessing her.

I asked if she would like to know the sex of the baby at delivery and whether she would want a cuddle, or if she wanted the baby to be taken away immediately. With great dignity and in a quiet voice she said she wanted to hold her baby and to know the sex before she handed her baby over to the social worker.

"You are in good hands and I will give you and your baby the best care, please ask me anything at all" I tried to reassure her.

"Is there anyone I can contact for you Shelley? A friend perhaps?" She asked. Shelley shook her head and avoided eye contact.

The room was very quiet, and as was my practice I kept the lights low. Progress was steady. The labour thus far uncomplicated, we were strangers meeting each other at the most intimate time, whilst life changing decisions were made. The mother very much aware, and the baby of course knowing nothing. Shelley's decisions had been made a long time ago. Only she knew the reason why she had to part with her child.

The delivery was normal and safe, and a new-born boy was gently escorted to meet his Mum. She held her arms open as I had seen many times before as she met her boy, soon to be passed into an unsure world. She didn't kiss or exclaim, the silence was loud, the baby cried, but the silence persisted.

Shelley had very little to equip the baby or herself. So, I went to the box of knitted garments, and chose, a vest, a white Babygro and a blue cardigan for him. I bathed him. Shelley watched. She didn't speak a word.

Within an hour the nurse from the special care baby unit accompanied by the social worker came to take the little boy from his mother. Shelley lay on the bed and watched him go in his little blue cardigan. I wheeled him to the door in his cot. The social worker looked back at Shelley and gave a gentle nod towards her. She left, and the baby was transferred to the Special Care Baby Unit, just around the corner from the labour suites. But a million miles away from Shelley.

I returned to help Shelley have a wash and make her some tea and toast. Shelley never spoke only to nod yes or no to any of my questions. Time was moving quickly, it was evening by now, and my shift was ending. The night duty midwives were soon to arrive.

I was ready for duty early the next day. I was wondering about Shelley, and I had slept badly. Her situation keeping me awake, as so many situations did over the years.

I went to ask the Sister in Charge how Shelley was, and was asked to sit down. All the staff were asked to sit down. She informed them that Shelley had left the hospital and taken her baby with her, she had gone to see her baby boy during the night and asked for another hold of him, just one more cuddle she had said. And then she took him, boldly walked from the hospital, wrapped in her coat, the close circuit television could clearly see them, but no one had stopped them. The police were looking for them both, the only thing left was a little blue cardigan discarded in the bottom of the cot.

I never saw Shelley again and never heard any more of the story. I hope that her life had somehow turned out.

There is no love like a mother's love. It is the most precious of all love.

Mutilated

A lady of African heritage was placed under our care one morning in the Labour Suites. She was married and this was her first baby. As a rule of thumb all first-time deliveries take much longer than subsequent deliveries. As with some culture's, modesty was a more important to her than most. I used to sometimes see this in the clinics. The ethnic ladies would give permission for the midwife to palpate her uterus but would only allow just enough skin to be touched. This made the job more difficult, yet modesty was more important than anything else. By its very nature midwifery is an intimate profession. I was the second midwife for this delivery. This was Fran's case. A highly experienced midwife. The lady's name was Elsa. She was modest. Shy. Frightened. She constantly sought reassurance from her husband. They spoke their own language. Sometimes in the labour room, the midwife was the outsider sometimes she would be central. The labour progressed and I taught her how to use the Entonox, this is commonly used in childbirth, is effective and of course is fifty percent oxygen, and it crosses the placenta thereby benefitting the baby in utero. She was shying away from the pain; she didn't seem to be able to perform the rhythm that was required. To go with it. Adopt it. Follow it. Breath into it.

"Have you had baby" Her husband asked me.

"Yes" I smiled "I have two boys" This represented a badge of approval. If the midwife had had her own children, she had passed some kind of test. It was commonly asked by labouring women.

He nodded. Kept close to his wife. They talked in their own language. I worked, alongside my colleague I kept sharp notes and when it was time I left them for fifteen minutes as I went for my break. I no longer smoked. Thank goodness. I was free of the pull of nicotine.

When I returned the lady was whimpering and writhing behind her mask, she was in obvious discomfort. I tried to communicate with her, and my demeanour is one of calm, despite my pumping heart, I feel inner calm that comes with concentration.

"Do you think Elsa would like some alternative pain relief?" I asked her husband because Elsa could not or would not look at me.

"No" He answered firmly. "No, she manages"

I tried to explain if she wasn't coping with the pain the delivery would take longer and a little bit of analgesia would help relax everything and allow for a much more calm and receptive delivery.

He was having none of it.

"No no she be fine with me here". I could see she feared him. I didn't. But I feared for her. I begged to differ but only in my mind. I discussed it with Fran.

"Well she'll struggle, and it'll take a lot longer, let's see if we can try and get her to have something extra." Pethidine was the drug of choice in the nineties, it was an injection given into the thigh, and relaxation of the muscles could be seen usually within twenty minutes. It was important to give it at the optimum time.

"I'll have to examine her first check she's not too far on" Fran was considering how to best manage things. The thing with the Pethidine was that it too crossed the placenta and if it was given too late the baby may be affected and be sleepy at birth. I tried again.

"NO" he said. "I look after her."

I smiled patiently as I was wont to do. I feigned confidence, but experience had taught me that she wasn't fine and wouldn't be fine. We had a bit to go and the pathway needed easing.

"I'll have to check you over Elsa" Said Fran, "Make sure baby is alright in there and then we can make a plan. Will that be OK?"

Her mask could well have been glued to her face as she nodded her permission.

I asked her husband to step outside to maintain Elsa's dignity, but he refused. So, Fran prepared her equipment and applied sterile gloves. I asked Elsa to lie back a little and tried to reassure her. The baby was tightly held back by Elsa body, maybe this was due to Elsa's timidity and restraint. Fran was frowning as she almost jumped back from Elsa.

"OK Elsa we'll be back in a minute" Fran nodded at me urgently, she pushed me outside of the room.

"Jesus Christ Karen she's had genital mutilation. Baby's head is low, but she can't stretch out. She's had Female Genital Mutilation"

I stared at Fran trying to absorb what she said. "Are you sure?"

"Course I'm bloody sure, mind you I've never seen it before, but the anatomy is altered, and she's missing areas of vulva. It's crooked, it's raw, we'd better get someone down here quick. Get this baby born. You call them out I'll go back in."

I did and they came, and Fran was right, and Elsa cried and sobbed her way through the delivery, and I held her hand and he was on the other side talking in his own language. He looked down the whole time. He knew we knew. I felt shock. Her mutilated body had been cruelly butchered by someone, who knows who. An elder. A leader. A witch. A grandmother, I didn't know, I felt numb with shock. I had never witnessed female genital mutilation, only read about it, never expected to see it. It was only as the baby's head was pushing forward that it had become evident.

I hated how I felt. The injustice of this barbaric procedure the terror she must have felt, and of all the cultural differences some I will never understand I long as I live. I do not get it. I simply do not.

When the obstetrician returned to suture the lady, I was to assist him

We gowned up and made the preparations I gave Elsa the Entonox again and reassured her it was almost over for her. This was often the most barbaric procedure for me as it seems brutal that following all that, still stirrups are applied, and legs are wide open to allow the work to be carried out.

Just before the doctor began, the husband asked him to step outside.

Without any hesitation or reaction, the doctor followed him outside.

"Make tight. Extra stitch for me"

"What do you mean?" He later told me he knew exactly what he meant.

"Make good for me more pleasure for me." The doctor about turned without replying and continued with his work. What a world we live in I thought.

Leah

During my time of midwifery practice, it was sad and very worrying to observe the incidence of domestic abuse increasing during pregnancy. Of the numerous courses' midwives were obliged to attend violence from partners towards pregnant women was mandatory. This developmental course led the midwives to routinely question their clients if they were being abused or treated cruelly. I found it difficult to look someone in the eye and ask them if they were being violated in any way? And then expect an honest answer. Really?

Hello, my name is Karen I am your midwife for the next 9 months and are you being abused?"

I am being facetious I know but the changing world makes me this way, makes me sad and I want to be more worldly wise, but I resist it. I like my world. My bubble. Looking back everyone but everyone had problems, there were very few straightforward cases, who could just be, accept, relish and enjoy the experience.

We took it in turns to do the clinics and the visits. This day it was my turn for clinic and as ever it was busy. Each woman was allocated ten minutes. The clinic commenced at nine in the morning and was supposed to be completed by twelve midday.

In this time these tasks had to be performed.

1. Welcome chat
2. Any concerns
3. Is the baby moving (depending on gestation)
4. Blood tests needed (depending on gestation)
5. Blood pressure, urine testing, weight and depending on findings what would happen next
6. Palpation. Here I would determine the lie and the position of the baby, and measure whether the baby's head was descending into the pelvis. This was measured in fifths. If I could feel three fifths, then two fifths were engaged into the pelvis.

All being well done in ten minutes!! I learnt to juggle many balls in the air at once. I loved clinic, but it was mentally exhausting and if someone disclosed that they were being abused then it cannot be rushed. Women saw us as a confidante and that was our professional duty. We were there for her and the family.

I recall a young lady pregnant with her third baby. She was uncomplaining and quiet. I did the routine checks and then I asked her if she felt alright and if she had any concerns. She was ready to leave, putting on her coat and gathering up her other children. Little toys, dummies, bottles and lidded drink cups.

"I've been bleeding" she said as she stood up.

"Have you? Right Ok" I said, I had just palpated her and listened to the heartbeat, everything seemed fine.

I asked her to sit back down. I leaned into her. I knew her fairly well.

"Can you tell me about it? How much blood? A teaspoon, an egg cup, more less? Was it when you wiped yourself? Was it a gush? Was it just on the pad.?" These questions were geared towards getting a clear picture, and we were trained to question this way.

"About half a cup" She shrugged. "It's fine, I'm OK really. Only happened the once"

I didn't feel it was OK. I looked at her, her children, her lack of money and transport, and help.

"Where's your boyfriend today" Do you think he could take you to the hospital and get you checked out?"

She looked down and was reluctant to answer.

"I'll be fine" she said. My second brain was agitated. My intuition kicked in Things weren't right. I considered bundling them all into my car and driving them to the hospital, but I could imagine the managers face if that happened. I was floundering. The children were beginning to whine and tugging at her to go.

"I'm worried about you Leah. Why do you think you've had a bleed? If there's a good reason, then we can sort it. Sometimes it's the placenta, if it's low lying, sometimes there's a little area on the neck of the womb, there's any amount of reasons, probably nothing to worry about, but we need to check, lets get you to hospital and get a scan. It won't take too long."

"If it's nothing to worry about, no big deal" She looked into my eyes, gave a little affirmative nod and left. Children in tow.

I felt worried and disappointed in my lack of persuasion skills. I needed to see it through and ensure safety for her and her unborn baby.

I finished the clinic. It was past lunchtime, as usual I had run over time. I discussed it with the doctor, and between us we tried to contact her through the day to no avail. So, at the end of the day, I went to the address and knocked but got no answer. I saw fit to put a note through the door.

Dear Leah,

I hope you are OK. I have been ringing you this afternoon. I still feel concerned about you and baby. I wonder if you'd reconsider and go to be checked. If not, then I'll try and catch you tomorrow.

I signed my name. I thought I was doing the right thing. How wrong I was.

Her partner found the note and presumed that Leah had disclosed to me how she had started to bleed, and he beat her up again, which was how she'd been bleeding the first time. His anger increased as the pregnancy progressed. He was one of the statistics that I had been learning about. She bled again and this time had no choice but to be seen, as she went into spontaneous labour and was delivered of a little baby girl, at twenty-eight weeks gestation.

When I found out about this, I ostracized myself. I was full of guilt and sadness, and frustration. I was worried and anxious. I felt isolated. Overwhelmingly I took full responsibility. I let her down. I knew that by leaving the note I had escalated the situation which was fragile enough. I hadn't realised it. I found myself deep in thought and staring into space for hours. I couldn't believe my naivety I felt true remorse. It was new to me.

I was lightheaded and had never been that way before. Leah's partner had read the note and presumed she'd confided in me.

This situation cultivated a change in me. I recall it was this major episode that drilled onto me the importance of using my intuition instead of acknowledging it, and ignoring it, I needed to be wary of consequence. Ten minutes is simply not enough time for appointments such as these.

I learned with experience that people will only ever tell the professional what they want them to know. I could have coaxed, pleaded, requested, yearned demanded, but Leah didn't want me to know. Yet she mentioned it but could not emphasize things. She was stuck.

Social services stepped into Leah's life, and her circumstances, and her path in life changed for the better. The baby girl lived with special care, and I often wonder if she grew up to be as stoic and as steely as her mother.

The Kosovans

I was promoted to work in the community as a midwife in 1996, and I got stuck in. I had a brilliant mentor, whom I still meet up with. Celia who is older than me taught me most of what I know. She had a great manner of sharing her knowledge and she had a subtle wisdom about her. After she had retired, I carried her with me. Whispering in my ear whilst sitting on my shoulder.

"Do it this way or don't say that take your time or think about how you're recording it." I had and continue to have so much respect for her.

In 1999, May 20th, Ulverston had prepared itself to take 100 Kosovan refugees. They had fled from war torn Kosovo and were to be housed in the old Lower school. The preparations had been on going, and it was reported that it cost £2000,00 to transform the school. Old classrooms were made into small bedrooms. A makeshift launderette was set up, and the large old school dining room was well equipped to accommodate the families to allow them to all eat together.

"Karen, we have to go to the Old Lower School and see what we can do as one of the ladies is pregnant and can't get to clinic." Celia said. "I 've about as much idea as you, all I know is that we need to see her and find out as much as possible. Let's aim to include her and her partner, if he's here, see if we can get them into our system here."

Off I went. It was odd for me as I had attended this school for a time when we came to live in Ulverston. It was a good set up. There were two caretakers sitting at a makeshift reception desk, guiding people and any visitors, which was me that day. I was escorted to a small bedroom that had been previously a classroom. The room was very warm, and a young woman sat on the edge of the bed, a young man, her boyfriend I presumed sat in a chair in the corner of the room.

"Hello, my name is Karen and I am your midwife, I've come to see how you are, is that OK?"

Nothing, no smile. No response nothing. What was I expecting? These people had been ripped from their homes with nothing of their own to speak of, no English language, and stuck in a room. I stepped back to give it some thought. I said it again:

" I am your midwife." But this time I cradled my arms together as if I were holding a baby then I rubbed my tummy. I was making it up as I was going along. I saw a small smile, a little shy look, and a nod. I asked if I could sit down next to her.

I said "Are you OK.... ok? I was floundering really, just muddling on. Doing what I do best.

In due course I got my equipment from my nursing bag. My sphygmomanometer, my sonic aid to listen the baby's heartbeat, my sample testing for urine and all the relevant paperwork. I worked on, smiling and doing a bit of gesticulating and sign language in my own way, and we got the job done. I heard the baby's heartbeat; I checked her vital signs, and everything was fine.

Time went on very quickly as it does in pregnancy care, because everything is so routine. This is done at this time, we'll see you in a month, then a we'll see you in two weeks, then we'll see you weekly. We formed a bond, and I looked forward to seeing her. Her face was starting to relax a bit, and she made good eye contact. The baby was growing.

The centre was full and was beginning to smell a bit. Bags of washing waiting to be laundered and the children unwashed running around, older people declining to maintain their own personal hygiene probably down to their dignity being compromised. It was a strange and difficult time for them. If I visited on lunchtime that was good, everyone sitting together in the large hall, chatting and eating.... It was a loud affair. It reminded me of school dinner times. It felt comfortable. The people in charge had made language cards for use, they weren't a lot of help to me as none of them said is the baby moving at least ten times a day? do you feel well .... any headaches or swelling? But it didn't matter as I used my eyes, ears, and body language.

Eventually when the time came my lady went into hospital to have her baby. Once she returned to the centre, I was sent to give her post-natal care. She had a baby boy.

There were two moments that stood out for me. When I first visited her, it was swelteringly hot and the centre was looking worse for wear, although health professionals were doing their best as were all the volunteers. The place was dirty. It was difficult for the community to keep things ticking over. As I entered her little bedroom, she looked so proud and happy. She was laying on the bed. There was the baby in a makeshift crib, wearing a nappy and vest. To my horror his face was covered with a cotton cloth, and his little arms were tucked into him. I felt a rising panic and grabbed the cloth off his face.

"Don't cover his face, we need to be able to see him" I said.

She grabbed it off me and placed it on his face again and tucked it gently around him.

"I took it off again, He can't breathe I said, and its so hot in here" I was feeling a bit harassed.

She placed it on his face and picked him up, and looking right at me she said:

"In Kosovo if baby is boy makes strong for him, with cloth face. Look...... makes strong for him"

It took me a minute or two to realise what she was trying to tell me and then I clicked. This was cultural. This face covering was what they did if they had a baby boy. They believed that this cloth across his face would make him strong. Feeling uncomfortable I went with it. The cloth was safe enough and he could breath and he was thriving. Who was I to make any changes to her culture? Anyway, I was shrewd enough to know that it would be replaced when I left, even if I confiscated it.

There is a lot of law surrounding midwifery and post natally we could discharge a lady ten days following delivery, if there were any concerns, we could keep them on until day twenty-eight.

This little chap developed a cold, when he was about a fortnight old, and it was no surprise really. I felt a bit concerned so I decided to keep him on my list. When I got there raised voices were coming from the little room and the baby was crying. I knocked and entered. My lady was crying, and her boyfriend was holding the baby, rocking him.

"He OK now, he OK"

I waited for them to explain, in our jumbled way. As I understood it, the baby had turned blue as he couldn't breathe, due to his nose being so blocked. They had used this implement that was common in their country. It was a pear-shaped thing with a tiny funnel on the end. It was made from pliable plastic and when it was squeezed in and gave a sucking action. They had put the funnel to his nose, and it sucked out the secretions from the nose, the baby turned pink. He then cried a healthy cry. I was fascinated with this thing; we'd always worried as midwives because babies cannot blow their noses, and this was a sure way of helping him. The boyfriend opened a small bag and took another one of these from it and gave it to me.

"For you. Take" Once again I was humbled by the human spirit, they had nothing, and they shared with me. I've never forgotten the Kosovans It was an absolute privilege to be allowed to visit, they had many babies during their stay, and we frequented the old school countless times for ante natal and post-natal care. I loved it, because even though the circumstances were sometimes sad, there was a lot of love in there. That was proven with how many babies were made at that time! They were seeking comfort and warmth.

Some Kosovans lingered in Ulverston and some left to return to a safer homeland. I was proud to be part of that historical time, and I hope that they felt safe and welcome during their time in our town.

The Chart Lied

I was learning my profession quickly. The labour ward was consistently busy, and the clientele were varied We midwives needed to be adaptable and on the button. My work was becoming slick. Once over if a baby were about to be born, I would want to run out of the room, now, I was not leaving until my work was done and a new life was here. I looked forward to the deliveries and holistic approach that was encouraged.

And then I was moved to the Special Care Baby Unit. I felt that I was back to square one. My learning was to begin all over again. Here the babies were more dependent and round the clock nursing, feeding, temperature gauging and the balance between letting Mum and Dad have a cuddle and keeping hands off to allow growth and rest had to be negotiated. I loved it, I loved every minute of it and again I was acutely aware of the personalities of the staff, subconsciously choosing my favourites nurses to learn from lean on and be guided by. I knew that I would only be working here for several weeks, because things were changing and the move towards paediatric nurses, not midwives becoming the more valued and suited staff in this specialised area of work.

An ordinary day. We were busy we had triplets all stable, growing and feeding, and all doing well, one lagging but feeding hungrily and would quickly catch up. We had a new born gestation at thirty-four weeks and the sucking reflex not yet available, so she required tube feeding and making sure her temperature was stable. That was all really and as I left my late shift at nine thirty in the evening. I was to recommence at seven thirty the following morning.

All babies as all patients needed to be checked regularly. Some two hourly some three. Temperature, heart rate and respiration rate. Skin, for any redness bruising or fragility, and of course nappies and a record of fluid intake and output. Also, peripheries, nail beds, toes and fingers. It was around the clock job, very routine, and lasted twenty-four hours a day.

The following day, I went on duty, the night staff reported no changes, and left to go home to bed. I only had one baby to look after the little thirty-four-week-old baby. There were twins pending in the labour rooms, but not ready for delivery yet.

Having finished my coffee. My baby was due for a bath and feed, so I set to. I collected all the routine equipment and ran the bath and started to strip the baby off, keeping moving as to maintain her temperature. I removed her hat but as I tried to remove the glove off the left hand it seemed to be stuck. I gave a little tug, but it would not come. I investigated further and to my horror there was a ribbon from the mitten tied tightly around the baby's fingers and two fingers were black, the blood supply had been cut off, and as I tried to untangle the ribbon, the finger was going to drop off. It was completely necrosed. The fingers were dead.

"Sarah, come here" I shouted, through the glass partition. I could feel the sweat pouring down my back.

Sarah looked through the glass and held up her hand.

"Five minutes, I'm in the middle of it"

"No come now". Maybe she could hear the urgency in my voice, as she came tutting.

"What?"

I did not speak, and I held the semi gloved hand and showed her the little fingers black and crumbling inside the mitten.

"What is that? What the hell has happened?"

"I don't know"

"They can't have checked the hands overnight because it was all OK at nine last night"

"Well what does the chart say"

I got the chart. "It says checked. It says fine"

"Can't say that…give it me…"

Sarah grabbed the chart off me and stared at the ticked box. She stormed out of my glassed area and got on the phone.

Then all hell broke loose. The medical staff came and chief midwife clinical leads and managers alike. I remember I was told to go and carry on with the other work and look after the triplets who all needed feeding in succession.

I have never forgotten this devastating discovery and I checked in with an old colleague of mine and she too remembered it. It is the saddest thing, that little girl lost her wedding ring finger and the one next to it. From then on, all hand knitted clothes and garments were banned. The lovely knitting ladies were no longer, and all mittens had to be shop bought made of soft cotton and in sealed packages and a safety triangle on the packet. No loose threads in order to protect the little hands and feet of the precious new born.

This action represents what we see a lot of these days, a solution that isn't really a solution it's a blanket, a covering, an idea a notion, what really should have happened is that the staff should not tick boxes without doing the check. It is deceitful, lazy, dangerous and intentional. And very scary. Maybe staff should have a safety triangle printed on them somewhere.

I often think about the suing culture which is now virulent across the Western world and it makes me wonder and sometimes I sit and think and sometimes I just sit.

The Buddhists

The times I went to the Buddhist Priory as a midwife, are forever inside me and as I recollect and dredge up my memories, it's more about how I felt. I was in a place to learn, to continue soaking up the spirit of the human being. Don't get me wrong, when I was hands on working, I was always in the moment. When I was with a woman and her baby, I was right there, with her and nothing would ever distract me. I felt a real passion for the job. I was very fond of going to the Priory though, it put things into place for me. The peace. The quiet. The pace. Unrushed. Reflective and warm. It was a comforting place to be. The materialism of the world faded into nonexistence as I entered their world.

I had to leave my shoes outside the door, and that was fine. I soon learnt to have matching socks and no holes in them, although I'm sure only I would notice. Stepping over the threshold of the small adequate room my lady was lying on a mattress on the floor, her baby was wrapped in a shawl snuggled into her Mum. I could hardly believe the feeling I got from being there, I wanted to stay and be looked after myself, instead of me always doing the looking after.

It resembled being wrapped in a great big warm blanket of safety. Cocooned.

My life, forever dashing about had become a habit that was increasingly difficult to break. Colleagues, family, and everyone I met assumed that I would and could do it. I was here, there and everywhere. Clinic, home birth on call, labour ward beckoning and the constant questioning from anxious Mums to be. The idea that life was soon to be perfect. "That once I've had this baby everything will be perfect won't it won't it? My relationship will be sorted, money will be plentiful, my house will look like an advertisement from the television, I will be immaculate, slim and attractive again and my baby will be the best there is, best dressed, best pram, most expensive toys and equipment. Of course, my baby is clever I can see it already, very advanced. Very". Oh yes then the holidays. The Christmases the constant striving and call of the material world.

To be amongst the Buddhist ladies was refreshing beyond belief. The colour, the bedspread, the wall hangings, the pots and pans, every type of tea and coffee, and someone popping in to bring a meal and a hot drink, so Mum could concentrate on feeding her baby. Ultimately the peace, quiet and stillness. The feeling of stopping. Stop right there. Stop. I appreciated the lack, yet they appeared to have so much more than anyone else.

"It's no wonder their babies hardly ever cry. They've got it bossed in there." We commented to each other.

Sure, enough there was sometimes a language barrier, but it didn't seem to matter, even between themselves. The difference between the Kosovans and the Buddhists was a choice. The Kosovans had their choice taken from them; the Buddhists made their choice.

Often, we were surplus to requirements. The Buddhist ladies didn't use us much. They were attentive, gracious and thoughtful towards each other. They were self-sufficient and their belief of giving out into the world, they would receive back was all they needed at that time.

However, it was a legal requirement that we attended.

I loved going there. I was sent constantly within my midwifery practice, and I also went years later to visit the sick and dying. That too was a situation to be appreciated. Once again, it was to my benefit. The tenderness and gracious care were as strong. Non-invasive, but as always, this community were prepared to stand up and give what was needed, delivering at the optimum time.

There's Something Wrong with That Baby

A routine day in the beautiful lake district, despite the rain. I was sent to a visit in the back of beyond. Mum and baby were reportedly doing well, and the baby was a week old, and due to be weighed. I enjoyed the drive; I took my time and relishing being in my own world. It was my preference to be working alone. It was a gem of a job, and I treasured days like these.

I duly arrived. I remember part of our uniform were these awful gaberdines. Mine was too long because one size fits all and I am small, mine was down to my mid-calf. It was grey, the dullest colour and completely shapeless. When I entered the house, I took it off and folded it and as I was trained to do. Always that the outer layer of the coat was placed on any surface in the house, this way the inner layer that went next to my skin remained clean.

The young couple were adapting well to parenthood they had a little boy and had named him Billie. They were pleased with his progress, but his Mum mentioned that he had been sick a few times.

"Was it projectile?" I asked, "Did it seem to be forceful and go across the room, or was a little bit after a feed?"

"What colour was it?"

All the questions we are trained to ask. Mum replied.

"Not really, I think it was with a feed, but it happens after most feeds"

"Let's get him weighed that'll give us a good idea"

I stripped him off and placed him on my scales.

His weight I recall was steady. I did the maths. It was safe for new-born babies to lose up to a tenth of their birthweight by day four and then it was expected that that the weight would start to increase, providing there were no problems. Billie's weight was steady. No great weight gain, but no real cause for concern either.

I chatted with Mum about the feeds, I questioned her about how she was making them up, about sterilisation and about the types of teats that were available and checking that she was using the correct type.

I could not find any reason to be really concerned, but something was niggling me and my intuition was jumping around inside me. My second brain was at it again.

I said "I'll tell you what we'll do. I will pop back in two days' time and check his weight again. Meantime I have some contact numbers. You can use them day or night."

"Remember to sit him up a bit when you feed him, and watch out for him gulping it down. It would have been better if I could have observed your feeding, but he'll only feed if he's hungry and that's not right now."

I got up from the floor where I had been kneeling and started to pack my things up. When I was ready, I looked around for my dull gaberdine. Just as I was about to cross over to the sofa where I had left it, Billie vomited. I have never seen anything like it since or before. Copious amounts of thick, green, faecal smelling vomit, which flew across the room covering my clean folded gaberdine. It ran like a river onto the carpet. I grabbed the baby and held him face down whilst he vomited to make sure he did not choke or inhale any. Once the poor child had finished, he went a deathly white colour and lay very still.

I said "Now that was a vomit. Has it been like that before?" Mum shook her head. She was crying.

I said "I'm going to call the doctor get Billie checked over"

I rang from the house, as the mobile phone world was yet to be developed.

"Often, I said the doctor will prescribe Gaviscon or an antacid that will coat the sphincter at the top of the abdomen and prevent that forceful vomiting."

To be honest I was reassuring her as best I could nonetheless, I knew something was very wrong.

I rolled my gaberdine up into a ball, and then offered to wash the carpet where it had spilled.

The next day, I was on duty again. The first phone call I made was to the Billie's parents. There was no answer. I tried a few times then left it. Later, I phoned the surgery, to enquire if the doctor had visited and whether the problem was solved.

"Oh," said the receptionist. "I thought you'd have heard. The baby has a volvulus and malrotation of the bowel. He is in Manchester and has had surgery. He was rushed there in the middle of the night."

I thought I knew it was serious but had not realised how serious. This is a condition that develops in pregnancy. The baby's bowel is not formed properly and is twisted. It does not form into a coil in the abdomen and the part of the intestine is cut off from blood supply and it is a life-threatening situation.

The thing that struck me and has struck me time and again during my career, is the fact that I felt and continued to feel that I was being watched over. That vomit happened as I was preparing to leave, and it would have been missed if I had already gone. I have had so many situations that my gut has been nagging me to do something. to act on it. Now today. Not to wait not to leave it. Sort it now, and this was one of many times that I can recall.

Billie recovered well following his surgery. I threw the gaberdine away even though I thought the green colour was slightly more favourable than the grey! The represented colour of the community midwife in the nineties.

Time to go

Midwifery is an ancient art but however much technology is taking over our lives the body remains the same. Will robots deliver babies in the future? I hope not. Midwife means with woman. It is a deep and meaningful job and most people in life have children.

In the name of progress, the unit I was working in decided to cut the staff by half. This they said would be cheaper. Of course, it would. They said that if they were sued it would ultimately be cheaper than having to pay the staff as it was in 2006. Midwives they said, are expensive.

I was working the night shift with skeleton staff AGAIN. I was in the labour suites and I had with me two assistants. I can remember feeling particular tired, I was bringing up a family and work seemed to be becoming harder. I could concentrate OK but I was tired. Nights didn't suit me.

The ladies I was looking after were uncomplicated so far.

"How much longer do you think" my lady asked me between contractions

"You're doing great you're making really great progress, if you just keep doing what you're doing we'll see baby soon enough" I never committed myself to a time that I thought baby would be born, even if I had a good idea. Experience had taught me in midwifery circumstance can take you by surprise, and I've been taken unawares before.

She laboured on.

"Try and and have some water or some of that sugary drink, keep your blood sugar up. You know you'll need your energy later on." This was her third baby.

I went into the next room and my second lady was not fairing so well. It felt like a big baby, and her pain wasn't under control at all.

"How about some extra pain relief" I asked.

"MMMMM OK How much longer?" I thought I'll just lift my crystal ball out from under the bed, how rich would I be now if I'd had THAT gift!

I went to call on someone to check with me the controlled drug to administer to her. There was nobody about.

"Great one o'clock in the morning and nobody here" I went to pull the bell see if anyone could come and help me. Nobody came.

Then I heard a commotion

"Get her into special delivery. It's breech this and they never told us."

The word breech in midwifery is alarming to say the least. The rule is hands off, same as water birth hands off. I like my hands on carefully guiding the baby into the world. A breech delivery is allowed to 'hang 'so to speak. The baby's bottom, (known as a Frank Breech) or the legs (known as a footling breech) deliver first which ever is presenting. Then the body will follow,and lastly the head. It's dangerous because the head is the lastpart of the baby to deliver and the professional doesn't know, if the head will pass through the birth canal as it is the widest part and stretching hasn't occurred due to the softest part of the baby being delivered first. These days breech presentation is always a caesarean section delivery.

Of course, this lady over ruled my lady who required pain relief who overruled my other lady who needed me there. And there were only three staff and all the rooms were full of labouring women. In pain needing guidance. It fleetingly occurred to me that this was dangerous, and we were sinking. Looking back this went on for months if not years until disaster struck. But we didn't know this yet.

"Right we need you to work with us Yvonne, your baby is upside down and it's too late to go to theatre, so just listen to my voice and I'll guide you." The sister had come over from the ward to conduct the delivery. Thank God I thought

I had called the paediatric team and we were ready and as it happened the baby just slipped into the world cried straight away and pinked up nicely with no intervention necessary.

"Can someone check me some pain relief, Gemma in room two needs Pethidine"

We did that Gemma settled into a better more controlled labour which became rhythmic and focused.

"Can someone come to room 5 she's ready to deliver. So, we did that. Mum and baby fine. Midwife not doing so well. I hadn't eaten since I got up at four o'clock in the afternoon and it was now three o'clock in the morning. I was, as usual, running on empty.

"Karen your lady in room seven is shouting for you. I think it's her third?"I nodded and ran down the corridor.

"Help me out" she groaned "I can't stand it". A sure sign that she was almost ready to deliver. I needed to stay with her but there was so much going on outside of the room and I was needed there too. The night dragged on yet flew by. Nobody had eaten anything all night and this was the norm.

We had five normal deliveries and the breech lady plus attenders with blood loss and babies that weren't moving as well as they should. I was tired.

"Thank Christ it's morning" One of the assistants said "My bed is calling me" she yawned loudly.

I turned the computer on and sat down in preparation to input all the deliveries in detail.

I sighed to myself, I felt sad because in my heart, I knew it was time for me to start thinking about moving on. I knew I couldn't keep this up. It felt unsafe and the only changes there would be were going to make our roles as midwives harder and riskier.

Mr Prince a Royal Man

We are all born innocent and as life begins circumstance, opportunity and genetic history will play a part. Nature Nurture the argument is continually debated.

A man I looked after required daily injectable medication, he was unable to manage it himself. I didn't like him. I felt uncomfortable around him. When I went into his flat, I felt vulnerable and claustrophobic. The flat smelled and so did he. It was a worn-out kind of odour. Sour. Used up. Tired. I am sensitive to smell, but I accepted it and breathed through my mouth.

"Morning Mr Prince, How this morning?" Every day cheerful smiling, I used to think "Get in do the job get out" Keep breathing" Didn't like it. My manager at this time was great. She understood and was fair. She made sure the nurses shared him out. She had been a district nurse and I always felt great respect for a boss who had risen up from the shop floor, had worked on the ground. Over my career I was unfortunate to have managers that had never nursed who weren't nurses and presumed to understand the job.

We all took turns to visit Mr Prince. His life history was scant. We understood that he'd had a difficult start in life, and had suffered paranoia. He was resentful towards others. He blamed everyone for everything. But he was clever. I called it daft on the right side. He knew how to work the system and he was manipulative. He played one nurse off against another.

"That one yesterday she did it wrong and she didn't wash her hands for long enough"

Then "That fat nurse she didn't speak two words to me, do you know her, the fat one?"

I used to nod and plead ignorance as much as I could. And another thing there was always pubic hairs on the soap, it was almost like he'd left them there on purpose, then he'd watch as you tried to clean the soap, and as for the towel well that's another story. Of course, there was no hand sanitisers, liquid soap or kitchen roll in his house.

On occasion he was naked when I arrived hands on his hips, his pale waxy skin stretching across his abdomen and everything dangling and exposed, "Well aren't you coming in, shut that bloody door will you it's freezing"

"Well maybe pop some clothes on Mr Prince," I smiled at him. Then he would purposely squeeze past to get to his clothes. You get the picture?

Mr Prince had a built-up shoe. It was brown and he wore it to allow him to walk and get about, although he was terribly lame, and used two sticks. The shoe's platform was about four inches high. I was sad about his shoe, I wondered if during his limited school life, he was used and abused. He was not the type of person to share anything without twisting and lying. "Are you alright Mr Prince "I would ask him"

"Why wouldn't I be "he'd sneer back at me. But I never gave up until one day, when his cruelty shone through him like a beacon on a dark winter's night. I shiver when I think about it.

To get to the flat it was a small flight of stone steps. He lived at number nine, and directly opposite was number ten. I often used to see a cat waiting to get into number ten. He was a gorgeous animal, a big tom cat, black and white, a handsome lad. He was called Chips; on occasion I had spoken to the neighbour and so knew the cat fairly well. "He's a fighter is Chips" He can't help himself you know; he likes the girls you see. We smiled at each other. One animal lover to another.

The occupant from number 10 was there on this day. "How you getting on with him in there?" He was fishing for information and I knew it. "All fine"

I nodded and moved on. "Watch him Nurse, he's not all sweetness and light you now, I'd hate any of you lasses to get hurt by him"

"It's fine we're Ok. Thanks though. See you later" I left him to tend to Chips' wounds.

It was my turn to see Mr Prince I'd had a run of days off so I felt fresh and ready to tackle anything. I was at the bottom of the stone steps when I could hear raised voices.

" You've bloody killed him you low life."

"Don't know what you're talking about" I recognised Mr Prince's voice.

I felt like turning round and creeping away, but his medication had to be given on time, I made myself climb the stone steps.

"Hello it's the nurse is everything OK? "

"It's him nurse I warned you I knew he was bad but to kill my cat, murder my Chips, well I never thought that would happen, you bastard, I know it was you"

I was stunned.

"Mr Prince would you like to wait inside for me sir?" He liked being called sir. He thought he deserved that level of respect. He stepped inside. I pulled the door to.

"I'll pop back" I said to the neighbour.

I went into Mr Prince's flat.

"Did you kill his cat?" I couldn't help myself

"What of it?"

I could feel my tears.

"Why why? That gorgeous cat"

"I was sick of it squawking all night creeping about. I couldn't get any sleep. So, I poisoned it. Serves him right he always fed it outside."

I completed my work in silence. I could no longer talk to this man. I left and went across the way.

"Are you OK? I am so sorry."

"Do you know what happened?" He asked.

"No not really do you?"

"He poisoned Chips; I can't prove it but he was dead next to his feeding bowl this morning. I just know it was him. Bastard."

I gave him a hug I had to. I've never forgotten this.

Eventually they moved Mr Prince into a care home, where we still had to go in to give the medication. He continued to cause havoc, tell lies, and manipulate people and he was as cruel as ever.

Satellite Navigation

I was beginning to find it difficult to embrace the modern world. I used to wonder if it was necessary. I knew the answer was always yes, it is necessary, it is in fact essential. Having said this, I was the only nurse in the community without a sat nav. I had a map. Everyone else had a sat nav, one they could access on their phones somehow, and the smooth talker would direct them from the dashboard. You could almost hear them smiling.

The rest of the team either shook their heads or laughed at my lack of progress. Progress I wondered?

On duty during the summer, I was allocated a lady Mrs Newby, she required palliative care, and lived in a caravan. As a rule, the nurses went in pairs to dying patients to check medication and give care. We supported each other. Susie was the nurse who was allocated to work with me, she was newly qualified and we arranged to meet at twelve midday, at the said caravan. But midmorning I received a call out.

"It's Mrs Newby" said the receptionist, "her daughter has called in and she is being sick, they want you to visit sooner."

"No problem. Can you ring Susie and ask her to meet me there?"

I turned around and proceeded to where I thought the caravan was. No bossy voice from the dashboard to tell me where to go, but I found myself driving up and down. I couldn't find it, so I stopped and rang the family's home number.

"Hello, it's the district nurse I'm looking for you, I must have driven past. Can you guide me please?"

"Course we can love...... tell me where you are exactly.... haven't you got a sat nav? Bit surprised. Thought you nurses would all be given one of them marvellous machines."

"No, I'm sorry I don't," I say. "I am on the back lane, behind the main road going in the direction of the sea front, the sea is on my left."

"Right, well, never mind, come to the narrowest part of the lane, which is on the right, keep left and I'll be on the side road to wave you in."

I followed the instructions, and I could see Mrs Newby's son waving a big red flag in the distance. I had to smile, I turned in off the lane and saw the caravan which was camouflaged behind the trees.

"Hello" I said, climbing out of the car,

"I'm sorry to be late, my colleague will be here soon, and she'll find it quickly because she has a sat nav."

"Grand." said Mr Newby.

I was shown round the back of the static van. There were flies, lots of them, and a fly screen was stretched across the open door. In the same field there were four horses sheltering in the shade trying to rid themselves of the flies, flicking their tails and shaking their manes. We proceeded to enter via the screen.

The patient, Mrs Newby, was lying in a make- shift bed, on the floor and covered with a light sheet. She was retching and spewing black vomit, she was choking on it. I quickly applied on my gloves and rolled her head gently to one side. The tar coloured vomit trickled out of the side of her mouth and down her nightdress. Once she had got rid of it, she relaxed a bit, and her breathing steadied.

I wondered where Susie was. I could do with her here I thought. I smiled and asked where the medications were.

"Here Nurse, in this box"

There were two plastic boxes both full of equipment. The room was small and cluttered. Trying to navigate my way across the room around the mattress was a bit of an obstacle course.

Still no Susie.

I drew up the anti-sickness medication and gently administered it into her thigh through a butterfly needle that had already been inserted by a previous nurse.

Still no Susie. Then, Mrs Newby let out one big sigh and died. Just like that. With me there still holding the syringe and needle, and still no Susie. And there I was with a dead woman who I'd never met before, in the heat of the summer in a caravan, with black bloody vomit, and flies trying to get in and no Susie.

I took my phone from my pocket and rang her.

"I know I know" she said straight away, "it's my sat nav it's taken me to the beach!" I was speechless.

"She's dead Mrs Newby's dead.... she's just died. "I said, in a low urgent voice.

"Oh God" she said" I can't find it give me some directions." So, I did.

Mr Newby waved his red flag again, as Susie arrived.

"All the nurses are getting lost" he said, "Still you're here now".

We looked at each other and held our nerve. And kept smiling. I stepped outside through the fly screen the Velcro grasping my hair as I passed through it. I was a bit sweaty what with the weather and the situation. I tried to compose myself.

The whole family were waiting outside.

I said to them all "I am so very sorry to have to tell you, but your lovely Mum has just passed away."

I was met with a loud silence, and then a sharp gasp from the daughter, she said,

"Can I be with her?"

"Of course."

We walked back into the caravan and she knelt to her Mum and gave her a little kiss, stroked her hair then wiped her own eyes. She got back up, saying she wanted to smoke, she would wait outside.

I said "Can we make your Mum comfy and give her a little wash? Is it OK if we cut her nightdress off and put a nice clean one before everyone comes in?"

The daughter said that would be fine. "Do what you need to do"

We set to. Susie found a bowl and went to the out house to fill it, and realising there was no hot running water, put the kettle on to boil. I gathered necessary things soap, sponge, tooth brush and I gently removed Mrs Newby's teeth.

Her face had a peaceful look about it, and when Susie joined me, we gently washed and changed Mrs Newby, cleaned her teeth, and carefully manoeuvred them back into her mouth. Anyone who's ever had to replace teeth into a dead person's mouth, will understand. I combed her hair and we changed the sheets. We worked on our knees, and by the time we had finished she looked clean and restful.

Susie went to ask the family to come back in the room. After a while some quiet crying was heard. Susie and I went into the outhouse to write our notes and give the family some space. After about five minutes the daughter came to us and said:

"My Mum doesn't look right. It's her hair, she never had it like that." She said.

I nodded and as usual I waited patiently.

"Can you put her these curlers in?" She showed us a handful of pink curlers, ready for us to curl Mrs Newby's hair. Susie looked at me.

"Of course, "I said.

We went back in, got down on the floor and each of us put six curlers in, once we had fathomed out how to do it and stop them from springing open! We checked with the family that they were appropriately placed and then we left. Once we were out of hearing we laughed like mad. Then Susie adjusted her sat nav ready to find her way to visit the next patient. Me I plodded on without one, and I continued to use a map until I retired.

Gary

All nurses have some areas of the body that they find harder to deal with than others. For instance, the homeless gentleman whose toes nails were so long and dirty they curled around his toes and dug into the bottom of his feet causing sores. You could smell them before you saw them. That was quite a common sight. It literally made my toes curl. My area of fear and distaste are the eyes.

Working out in the community suited me. I was, and continue to be, independent and self-sufficient. I was brought up that way. 'There's your feet stand on them,' was the saying in our house. My main downfall was my map reading. I just couldn't get it. Turning the map this way and that, to try and decipher left, right or worse still third left or right. Working in the town was somehow worse for me as I frequently drove up the one-way streets, twice I was followed by the police and cautioned. I didn't get it;I thought my way was always quicker and safer. The countryside was easier for me, as often the said property was the only property, and one could go no further as the road finished there.

One afternoon, I was allocated a new patient who lived in the middle of the town. A young man who had had a tumour removed from behind his orbital space and hence had to use a false eye.

I can recall as a student nurse going to Christies Hospital in Manchester and visiting the prosthesis department. The room was full of false limbs, noses, ears, hands, feet and drawers full of eyes. I remember pulling open a drawer when I thought the person showing us round wasn't looking and eyes of all colours, eyes staring back at me unblinking cold and extremely shiny. Many years later I enjoyed and laughed out loud as Mrs Doubtfire transformed herself with female attire, a suit in the female shape and a false face, it reminded me of that room at Christies.

I found the house, no problem, with the patient waiting for me to teach him how to cleanse and insert his false eye, I knocked, walked in shouting.

"Hello, It's the nurse, can I come in?"

I was greeted by an overweight golden Labrador, who was friendly enough, but immediately showed off by lying on the floor and licking his parts in a noisy and slobby fashion, once he had completed his task, he rolled over and rubbed himself all over the carpet, before he eventually stood up and shook himself, dog hair flying all over the room. Then he stood to one side and let me through. Now I am a dog lover, I love dogs more than people, but somehow this ill-mannered mutt did not register high on my likeable list. I stepped over him and made my introductions.

The young man in question, was patiently waiting for me and was well prepared. He had got everything ready on the table and the eye, green in colour was in the solution ready to be inserted. Having washed my hands, the dog following my every move, I opened my sterile pack I applied my gloves and apron and gently tried to pick up the slippery eye from the bowl. It took me a little while but once I had a firm grip and I felt confident, I gently persuaded the ocular space open with my free hand and the eye simply slipped neatly into the hole. The man didn't speak at all and I could feel the dog's breath at my side the whole time. Fortunately for me the prosthetic eye seemed to jump into the space, where the real eye had previously been, almost as if it was being sucked in from the inside, and in it stayed. My relief was palpable.

"Are you ok? How does that feel?"

"Yes, feels fine, I think. Just give me a minute to let it settle".

And it did, so I left saying I would see him tomorrow.

The following day I was set to insert the eye again with a view to teaching the patient and his wife how to do it so that they could become independent. I have to say I felt very nervous about this, I don't know if the dog unnerved me, or if because it was such an unusual case and I wasn't used to the procedure and I hadn't really been taught anything about it, I just followed my instinct and pretended I knew exactly what I was doing, which I didn't. And the fact was I hated anything to do with the eyes.

That night I couldn't sleep I kept thinking about the false eye and imagining I dropped it and the whole household erupted as it rolled underneath the sofa, I couldn't reach it and it kept winking at me. My mind was simply running away with me, I was dreading the visit. However, as I was taught by my Mum and trained by my seniors, I put my best foot forward. I got to the house, knocked and walked into chaos, there was hell on, my patient was shouting at his wife,

"Get hold of that animal and get it off him." His language was choice, and I choose not to use it here.

It appeared the dog had stolen the eye and was rolling it around in his paws picking it up with its mouth and throwing it in the air as dogs do, when in full swing of their game.

Now I like to think that in my working life, I am very much in control of whichever situation presents itself, but I can recall many times feeling what I call the 'Mad March Hare Feeling', in other words, run. Run like the wind and I felt this way that day and it reminded me of the, the man with the one lung who threw a snake onto my back for a laugh. But that's another story. Anyway, I tried to grab the dog whose name I heard being screeched across the room, was Gary. I had no chance he was loving it; he was in his element.

The three of us had no choice but to stand and watch and wait. It took a little while but eventually Gary settled himself, he got bored, he was breathless he lay down and dropped the eye, both the wife and I went to grab it and she managed to keep a tight hold of it. I caught my breath and went to wash my hands again and taking the eye from the wife checked the damage. It was fine no harm, barely a scratch. I washed the eye and inserted it into the solution left it to soak for a while to make sure it was clean.

My patient the young man, composed himself and said he would have a go himself with his wife overseeing him. It went well, they seemed to be a good partnership and the eye settled nicely in the space.

Naughty Gary stood and watched and as I cleaned up my things and put my coat on to leave, he started on his parts again. I could hear the slobbery sound. Once he had completed his task, he looked up at me, he seemed to be grinning, our eyes locked, and I swear he was laughing right at me.

The pills are too big

I was assigned to visit an elderly gentleman who lived on the smart side of town. I was looking forward to it. I loved the gardens there.

I was primed by the senior nurse before my visit. This gentleman had an abscess drained from his anatomy, and it was almost healed but needed checking. She also told me that he had attempted suicide whilst in hospital and safeguarding was in place. He was eighty-four years old.

"He is one of the thousands of people who have had useful and full lives but now in old age is lonely redundant and cannot see the point of being alive anymore. This is what he had told the mental health team following his overdose. They said he's alright now but imagine trying to take your own life at that age, it's so sad, he's a lovely man. Just in case he wants to talk you're prepared."

"Right thanks"

He lived in an enormous house with a huge garden which was wildly out of control. Lush trees and hedges, flowers desperate to be dead headed. Conifers big enough to be Christmas trees and pussy willow, wisteria and buddleia covered with butterflies. Bird feeders with goldfinches feeding tidily as they do. My kind of garden I thought. This is a gem of a job.

I knocked loudly. No answer. I tried the door. Locked. I knocked again. Nothing. I made way around the back through the jungle.

I entered through the back door

"Hello it's only the nurse can I come in" I shouted.

"In here nurse" a tired weary voice replied.

I saw an old man bent over in his worn leather chair. Next to him he had three toy border collie dogs in a make shift basket. I was used to seeing this a lot with the elderly people, soft toys representing their live animals in younger years. It was common.

"My name is Karen I just need to check you over today sir. Were you expecting me?"

Yes.

"Right well I just need to check your notes please" He made to get up. "I can get them if you point me in the right direction"

"I'll get them" He staggered across the room, and found them underneath a pile of newspapers.

I glanced through them catching up and checking everything was as it should be. He sat quietly in the corner. His toy dogs unmoving and silent in their basket. No television or radio to disturb the stillness in the room.

"I just need to check that the abscess site is all healed and sorted Mr H would that be alright with you?"

He staggered up from the chair again. The abscess had been in a private place on his body. He started to undress.

"Would you like me to draw the curtains? I asked

"No Lass just get on with it" I applied my gloves and checked. It all looked absolutely fine. Clean, dry and heathy.

"Looks fine Mr H all healed and done. You can get dressed again Sir." He struggled to get his feet into his trousers and stumbled a bit. I reached out to steady him and our eyes locked. I looked away first, feeling humbled by this man who displayed great dignity. He finished getting dressed and sat down his bones creaking their way into the old chair.

"Is there anything else I can help you with "I asked.

"Well I do have another problem he said. I waited patiently. Thinking "Here we go" I took a deep breath.

He leant across to the mantlepiece and reached for his pipe. He tapped it on the stone surround. Then he filled the pipe with fresh tobacco and struck a match to light it. It took a couple of goes.

I heard him sigh deeply. Time was ticking so I decided to see if I could chivvy him along saying,

"Is it about your sadness and what happened?"

He looked a bit put out and puzzled. I waited feeling I was getting things wrong.

"No Nurse I don't know what you mean by that. But I am worried about the size of these antibiotics, they're like bloody horse tablets, I'll tell you now lass I've never seen tablets as big. I wouldn't even ask a horse to take tablets this size. He was up again showing me the pills. They were big. I must admit. But I was so surprised about what he said I felt like giggling. I was prepared for an in-depth conversation about the state of the world and the people who live in it, and how we're all doomed … and the sad state of the loneliness of old people. That was not to be.

"Don't worry about the tablets I'll have a chat with the doctor see if you need a different one or if you no longer need them. It's been lovely to meet you." I left contact numbers and said I would be in touch.

The Doctor agreed there was no need to take the antibiotics and so I phoned him and that was fine.

Two weeks later Mr H checked himself into the local nursing home to be cared for, he lived there for two weeks only when he died. He was peaceful and he had his basket of toy dogs next to him.

Guide me

As District Nurses we rotated into the clinics to perform wound care for the able bodied. That is the people who were not housebound. First the nurse would be allocated a list next, she attended caring for people whom she had never met, knew very little history, and she worked alone.

Again, resilience autonomy and independence were the necessary qualities running the clinic to time in an unfamiliar area. I liked the clinic, it made a change, and most of all during my time I liked not having a computer. I worked as a nurse with no distractions.

This particular Saturday morning I was busy and the queue was predictability long.

I was nearing the end of my list when young lady knocked on the door, asking if she could have a word with me.

"I have had a breast lump removed, they thought it was something sinister, turns out it was an abscess" She said "It's been really sore and it won't heal, but I can feel something in it"

"What like? "I asked, "Another lump or soreness? Describe it to me."

"It feels hard and sort of thin and stiff somehow" she said. She was rubbing around the area.

I thought well she's a stranger I have no notes no history, she's walked in off the street, she could be anybody, with anything. And for the first time I remember wishing I had a computer to enable me to look at her history and do a bit of detective work, so that I could help her. Yes, Me wishing for a computer.

I invited her into the clinical area with her partner whom she wanted to stay with her.

I introduced myself properly.

"I am just standing in today in the clinic as it's weekend, but I can have a look and see if I can put some light on the situation. You're obviously worried. Let's have a look."

I asked her full name and Date of Birth and other formal details.

"Well Julie if you take your top things off, that'd be great"

Once Julie was undressed, she sat quietly on the edge of the bed. She had a dressing on her left breast which I gently removed.

Sure, enough there was evidence of an infection that had not yet cleared.

"Were you given any antibiotics?"

"Yes" She said "Flucloxacillin I've got a few left, I have to take them for three weeks" she said.

"That's good you need to carry on with them and complete the course. Now just point or show me where it's sore".

She ran her hand along the top of her breast area. I looked closely. I couldn't see anything.

She insisted "Look here"

I looked again and no nothing.

"Feel here" she said.

With a gloved hand I gently ran my hand over the top of her breast. Sure, enough I felt something sharp and pointed, but still I was unable to see anything.

I sat down next to her as I was wont to do when I was stuck. My brain ticking my gut talking again. I stood up and gently I ran my hand over her small body. Her smooth skin was interrupted by a sharp prick again. Still nothing to see.

"Can you lie down for me please Julie" I asked. "Sorry" I said, "I just cannot see anything but can feel something sharp and thin like you said".

She climbed up and lay down. Her position must have made a difference because as she was horizontal a steel point stuck out from the wound in her breast. My heart sank. I got my customary butterflies, fluttering inside of me. It was a metal guide wire; I was sure of it. The surgeon had failed to remove it following surgery. The guide wire was as it sounded, it guided the surgeon either with the use of the ultra sound scan or the mammogram, to the diseased area thus the surgeon could work in the affected area.

"What do you think Karen?" She said

"Not sure I answered when I was absolutely one hundred percent sure. I am going to have to ask the doctor"

Now on a Saturday morning finding a doctor who could just pop down to the clinic, was a feat in itself. My patient and I would be the least important clients. I decided to ask in the Accident and Emergency area.

They ran with it, they deemed it as important as I did and they arranged for the medical staff to see Julie and arranged an Xray.

I had two more patients to see. Apologising repeatedly about my delay, I saw them both and closed up the clinic, taking the key to the office.

As I was leaving, I heard someone shouting.

"Karen we've been waiting for you coming out of there. There was this wire inside of me I think they left it in, we knew it was odd didn't we Jim?" He smiled nodding his head. Their relief was tangible and quite honestly so was mine.

"Oh right, I wondered about that" I said, feigning surprise, "Have they removed it?"

"No not yet, I have to go back and have an ultra sound scan there's a queue".

There would be I thought, but you should go straight to the front of it. Of course, she didn't get to the front, but at least she was on the right track now.

I got into my little car, sighed, and got my list of patients out ready to get out into the community where I belonged.

A Wig and a Leg

One very hot day it was my duty to go into the Lake District for a nursing visit. I was asked to go and see a client who needed care with her urinary system. She could no longer pass urine herself due to disease process. Her catheter was supra pubic and needed changing. The catheter is inserted just below the pubic bone and reaches the bladder. This is an alternative route to passing urine which would normally be passed via the urethra.

I was warned by the other nurses that she disliked the procedure and was particular about who visited.

"But ignore that Karen, it's nothing personal, she's just a bit finicky."

The said patient lived on a farm in the depths of the Lake District. I relished being sent into the Lakes even in the Summer when it was heaving with traffic, caravans and motorbikes. It was the best job in the world I used to think.

It took a bit of finding, and I deliberated getting out of the car as the dogs were circling and barking noisily. It made me wary. I used to feel worried about farm dogs and have on occasion been told off.

"Thought you were never going to get out of that car lass" The farmer would often comment, usually with a glint in his eye.

I found the keypad and let myself in.

"It's the nurse hello......hello"

"Aaahh in here nurse" A shout from the back room.

I made my way in. The old farmhouse was built of stone and entering the building felt cool and welcoming.

I found her in bed in a corner of the room. I looked and looked away and looked again. She was stark naked, with no covers on and was completely bald. And she only had one leg. Her stump lolloping flimsily knowing it had lost its purpose.

I dug out my smile and stuck it on my face.

"Hello, my name is Karen, I've been sent to help you with your supra pubic catheter."

"No no never mind about that, I need other things, get me dressed and I'll need my leg strapping on, and what about my wig, get it...... it's on the dressing table."

I looked over to where she was pointing, sure enough what looked like a dead badger was plonked on the dressing table amongst the spilt talc and various creams and perfumes.

"Get it Karen ......it's there, it is Karen, did you say? Go on get it." She was pointing to the wig and she was getting a bit perturbed. Pointing and shaking her fingers and hands.

I did as I was asked. I picked it up. It was matted and smelt foisty with a hint of stale urine about it. I ventured back towards her, wig in hand. I felt as though I was being sucked into a situation where I didn't belong, but I was unable to stop it.

"No no you haven't brushed it. Brush it will you. Give it a brush"

I did exactly as I was told, almost in a daze, I held the offending wig in one hand and brushed it with the other. The brush I picked up looked like it had groomed every sheep on that farm.

"Not that one the one next to it" I looked to the dressing table and located the other brush which looked even worse. It was filthy and completely clogged up with hair.

I followed her instructions. I felt as though I was on automatic pilot. I brushed the dead badger and gave it to her to put on.

"Mirror, girl, pass me the mirror"

I gave her the mirror and caught my breath, glancing surreptitiously looking at my watch. I'd already been here over thirty minutes. The whole visit should only be that amount of time and I hadn't even started.

"Right "she said "Me clothes on that chair and I'll have a lick and a promise today"

I kept obeying her. There seemed to be no alternative. I washed her I dressed her, she had a pole above her bed that was a permanently fixed to the wall, this way she could lift herself up and down whilst I helped her with her clothes.

"Good. Good lass Karen, you did say Karen was your name, didn't you?" She repeated herself.

"Yes, Karen that's right"

"Right Karen my leg, put my leg on for me" Her authority was something I could not ignore. I was duty bound to continue. I put her leg on for her and I followed her instructions that were shouted into my ear.

I stood back. She looked like a completely different person. I'd done a half decent job, I thought, but I still hadn't done her catheter.

"We'll have a coffee now Karen" she said "Two sugars for me, you know how I like it"

That was the first clue that I thought she thinks we've met before.

I made her coffee and I made myself one too. I thought, "I'm late I might as well be late with a decent cup of coffee inside me."

"Hello Jean, It's only us, sorry we're a bit late". There were two people coming in I heard them whilst I was brewing up in the kitchen.

I looked out from behind the kitchen door and realised they had uniforms on! They were the carers! They had come to wash and dress Jean. I couldn't believe it.

"Oh" I heard one of them say. "You're already done. How come"

I stepped forward holding two cups of coffee.

"I've sorted her out"

"How come" she said again.

I felt so foolish "She told me to"

"I bet she did" The other one said.

I fell silent, I'd been worked, and I fell for it. There was no time left to do the catheter, I had to leave. I was embarrassed.

I left my coffee and gathered my things together.

"Bye Jean"

"Bye Kate it is Kate isn't it?"

She winked at me and I could see the glee in her eyes. Old Devil. The catheter would have to wait for tomorrow.

Mr and Mrs

My first nursing placement was with the elderly and my last post is currently working with the elderly. A couple were admitted to the home together. They had no family and had had a long marriage. The wife who I will call Mrs had a confirmed diagnosis of advanced dementia. She was aggressive and loud.

"Come on love eat it up and then you'll get strong."

Her husband insisted on feeding her, she had porridge stuck in her beard, nobody could get near her to deliver personal care, it was a vicious circle. Her nails were long and dirty. Again it was a brave staff member that risked being clobbered just as the nail clipper was ready to go. We ensured all risk assessments were in place and kept her as safe as we could. Her husband refused to believe that she was so ill.

"If you lot had a bit more patience and understanding, you'd be able to see she wants that food, it's you lot you don't know how to look after her, you're bloody clueless all of you. We were alright at home, before you came interfering. Have you any idea how much it's costing me, us being in here.... have you?" He repeated this many time throughout the day.

"I've worked all my life and for what? To pay .... for this.... the government this and the government that." On and on he went.

We cared for Mrs around the clock, we listened to her howling, swearing and we put up with being scratched, bitten and generally abused. When she was doubly incontinent it took five staff members to preserve her dignity, all the while dipping and diving and trying to avoid being the one in the firing line. One person tried to hold her hands as gently as possible to stop her from putting them in the faeces and urine, as we cleaned her. It was a full-on affair. Mr would be hovering over us. Watching like a hawk.

"She won't want that nighty on, she hates that colour and aren't you going to put her cardigan on, not that one the pink one and she hasn't had her breakfast yet , leave her alone, I'll let you know when she's ready. You lot really are the limit" Then "Have you any idea how much it's costing me to keep us in here? Have you? Daylight bloody robbery" He said "I've worked all my life, and end up in here paying for this, I've been frugal and thrifty and put my pennies by and for what........ paying for this that's what"

He stood in the way waving his stick, it was red hot day he had the thickest biggest overcoat on you've ever seen, the nurses and carers were sweltered hoisting, lifting manuvere in the small room, and coping with the smell on a hot summer's day. It was a tough day's work if Mr and Mrs were on your allocated list. Thirteen hours doesn't exactly fly by.

I felt sad for them both but especially Mr. He was so hurt and confused by the injustice of his situation.

"We've never had a holiday, never, no we saved it we thought no, no holidays for us"

"Well what did you used to enjoy doing Mr?"

"Enjoy enjoy, we weren't here to enjoy ourselves, we worked and stuck at it together, not like now the young ones spending all the time, holidays, fancy cars something new every five minutes, there's a couple on our street they go to that Centre in Manchester, when they get back they can hardly carry all their shopping, trainers they call them at £100 a pair they reckon. On the same day they have their hair done, she has her nails done then they have their tea out and a glass of wine. I bloody despair." He shook his head to show how bad it all made him feel.

"Oh, I said sounds like they know how to have a good spend and a good time" as I moved on to my next patient.

Mr and Mrs had been with us about a month and nothing much had changed; Mr still waved his stick and continually shouted his disapproval of everything and everybody. Mrs grew thinner and her flailing limbs were losing their strength to hit out at us.

One morning as I came on duty, the night nurse said: "Mrs has died, she died about three am, we went in to change her and she'd gone"

My first reaction was does Mr know.

"We woke him to tell him, but he doesn't believe us, called us liars and went back to sleep"

"Okay" It was going to be a difficult day. We got our handover and the night staff went home to get some sleep.

I went to see Mr straight away. I sat down opposite him.

"Hello Mr" I said, "I'm so sorry to hear that you wife died in the night". I got hold of his hand. He pulled it away.

"I let her down" He started to cry. "I was hard on her and now she's gone" His voice had risen an octave or two as he tried to compose himself. "I let her down, she wanted a family I said no. Not yet. Then it was too late She wanted to go on holidays and I said we couldn't afford it, she wanted to have some time away and I said we're alright here at home. And now she's dead. I let her down. I made her do what I said and now I can't tell her, and we can't go anywhere, it's too late."

I was quiet for quite some time, because to be honest, if it was true, then yes, he had let her down, badly and yes it was too late.

"I'm sure she didn't think that Mr" I said, "She loved you and it seems to me you had a lovely life together, you were obviously very close. It is always harder when you've been so close and there's only been the two of you. I was once told that it is the price you pay for loving someone."

We stared at each other for a while. I got up to leave him and start my jobs, leaning in and touching his hand again.

"I'm on until tonight, we're all here for you, you can come and find anyone of us, and we are here." I said.

Mr continued to stay with us despite the cost, which he resented so much. He had to sell his house. We were told, when the house was emptied by the authorities, they found over 50,000 pounds stashed in a tin underneath the bed.

Coronavirus

As I write this I am at the end of my career. I had the opportunity to take my pension. I wanted to start my own business whilst I still have some energy. I wanted a little pet shop. My love of animals precedes me and to be honest if I had my time again yes, I would be a nurse ...a vetinary nurse. The pet shop never came to fruition. Yet now I'm glad, as the economy has collapsed and the small businesses are sinking. We are in the midst of a pandemic. Corona virus has spread across the world, and has killed hundreds of thousands of people. People of all ages. People with or without underlying health issues. The world has come to a standstill and our National Health Service was ill prepared.

The place I worked had the required Personal Protective Equipment, and it wasn't an acute area. I felt we were updated regularly and the rules were clear. As soon as we entered the building everybody in the foyer had to dress appropriately, to protect ourselves and of course our residents. Aprons gloves goggles and masks. Hand sanitisers were plentiful and all hand washing facilities available, also all rooms were equipped with mop bucket and solution as per instruction. All crockery and eating utensils were soaked in the solution and left in the room for the required amount of time. Dirty laundry stayed in the en suite bathroom for seventy-two hours, in a sealed, red bag. After that time, we were to take it to the laundry area. We were allowed to take the protective clothing off during our break and that was a relief. The staff room was relocated to a much bigger room to allow distancing; however, it is impossible to give personal care to anyone from a distance. The incidence of positive tests was high in spite of the protection.

The saddest thing was the lack of contact that the residents had with their families and the other residents, it is so lonely and the lack of social contact affects the wellbeing altogether. More especially in a nursing home.

Some residents refused to take notice of "this daftness"

"I've lived through the war; this lot doesn't scare me"

"I know" I said "But what about everyone else. We're all in this together you know."

"So, they reckon, but it doesn't wash with me."

We did what we could. People died but maybe they would have died anyway? Maybe it was their time? It was the relatives I felt for in that situation, because at the beginning the testing was sketchy and not reliable, and the relatives wanted to know if their loved one had died of Covid 19. Also, they could not be with them as they died, although eventually that rule was relaxed a bit. The undertakers had their work cut out and again they had to protect themselves, and funeral attendance was sparce again adhering to the rules.

Nobody in the medical field has ever seen anything like it. I wondered if we have been neglecting our own hygiene. I can remember a time when we had to show Matron our hands before going on duty. Obviously, there was nothing to see, but boy we made sure we washed them properly. Just in case. Sometimes I see beautiful young girls and women in the toilets in the pub or restaurant go to the loo and come out and not wash their hands! Scary. Their hair and faces are immaculate but the hand washing doesn't happen.

The media reports that the government knew about the forthcoming virus but had delayed in preparation. As a consequence, the frontline staff had very little personal protective equipment, not enough staff and 43,000 unfilled nursing vacancies, they were lacking in foresight. They buried their heads in the sand. There was a national request for medical staff and nurses to return from their retirement to help combat this aggressive virus. I went to help and then I fell ill and tested positive for Covid 19. I developed a persistent cough which was different to my usual little cough, I felt tired and weak. Then I lost my sense of taste and smell. I felt that was quite dramatic. Next, I felt like a had the flu. Weak, aching and I had abdominal pain. I spent a lot of time in the hot tub, which was very soothing, but I did go to bed one day, feeling as though I just couldn't cope. I drank as much water as I could manage, and my lovely son organised some honey to be sent through the post for me as I often have honey in hot water when I am ill. It works for me. The fatigue that I have been left with following this virus has reached my very bones my very soul I would not have believed it possible. The tiredness is absolutely overwhelming. I sit down. I fall asleep. It's now five months since I tested positive. Corona has frightened everyone, it is such an infective and nasty virus.

Just when you think you've seen it all …

Clean as a whistle

This isn't my story, but I love it. It was told to me from an old colleague.

Years ago, district nurses gave baths to patients. This was usually a weekly occurrence and of course now this is a carers job.

An elderly gentleman was in the book for his bath this day (there were no computers, we wrote it down in a book).

Liz said she would go. She set off there was no problems, she got into the house, made her chit chat and bathed the man.

She then continued along with her other visits, until it was time to go in at lunchtime.

On her return her colleague, said "Mr Botham has rung in, he said he was waiting for his bath"

"I've been" said Liz.

"Well he's definitely rung,"

"Maybe it was before I got there because I've definitely been, mind you he never mentioned ringing up"

"What's the address?"

Liz gave the address she'd been to

Her colleague said "That's' the wrong address, who did YOU bath?!"

Sure, enough Liz had bathed the wrong man.

She said "Well he enjoyed it and I gave him a good do; hair, toes the lot"

They laughed and laughed. It's a true story and I wanted to include it; I smile every time.